We Ate Gooseberries

WE ATE GOOSEBERRIES

*Growing Up on a Minnesota Farm
During the Depression*

Fr. Vernon J. Schaefer

EXPOSITION PRESS NEW YORK

First Printing, January 1974
Second Printing, January 1978
Third Printing, October 1997

© 1974 by Fr. Vernon J. Schaefer

ISBN: 0-682-47836-9

Printed in the United States of America

To my Mother and Father, who worked and "fretted" through a difficult era of American history

Contents

Contents

Preface

There are still many people around who grew up on the farm during the days of the Great Depression. Many have moved to "town" since, but look back on their youth on the land with fond nostalgia.

It is for these people this book was written. Some others may be curious from a historical viewpoint about what farming was like then compared to what it is now. For them this book will provide a few snatches of that era.

Except for some of the autobiographical material in the front of the book, all this material appeared off and on in my weekly column over a period of several years. This column, entitled "Diary of a Rural Pastor," appeared in a church organ of the Diocese of Winona, Minnesota, **The Courier**.

It was in response to a considerable demand on the part of the readers that we put it all into book form.

Childhood Setting

CHAPTER I

Life Begins

Perhaps we should precede these vignettes of boyhood on the farm with a short autobiographical sketch.

A baby boy entered the world on a blizzardy day, December 30, 1919. The locale of this auspicious event was a windswept clapboard farmhouse on a hill in Cottonwood County in southwestern Minnesota eleven miles north of Heron Lake and ten miles northeast of Dundee.

This little fellow was gasping for breath like a fish on the beach, we're told, so his Aunt Fronea, who assisted with the grand entry of this wizened and purpling creature into the cruel old world, had some doubts as to whether it would survive. She put in a call to the nearest priest in order to get this fearful-looking creature signed up for the Kingdom before he croaked.

Father John B. Gregoire, of blessed memory, then pastor of St. Mary's Church, Dundee, braved the winter storm for a ten-mile journey to the farm of my honorable ancestors, Grandpa and Grandma Knott, where my immediate honorable ancestors, Mr. and Mrs. Joseph Schaefer, had taken up temporary residence.

Father Gregoire, a saintly priest if there ever was one, poured the saving waters of baptism over my head. He had no idea that some day he would have this little laddie as his assistant pastor at Sacred Heart Church, Waseca, Minnesota.

So, over the kitchen sink of that lonely farmhouse, I entered the ranks of the saints and found myself possessed of a somewhat uncommon nomenclature: Vernon Joseph Leroy Schaefer. I don't know why they stuck in this "Leroy" bit. I dumped it entirely later and shortened the rest to V. J. since I wasn't particularly fond of Vernon either. I don't know where Ma picked up that name. I doubt if she had studied enough history in that Oaks Lake country school to have found out about Mt. Vernon.

Anyway, Vernon wasn't a saint's name, and the Catholic clergy

were a bit sticky about things like that in those days, and even
the name of the residence of the father of our country would
hardly be regarded as exuding the required sanctity. If the bap-
tizing priest had been anybody but Father Gregoire, he might
have dumped the name right then and there after pointing a
lanky finger at Pa and reminding him of the wishes of the
Church to grace this lad with the name of a chap now happily
humming in Heaven and who might also be able to pull a few
strings in behalf of the little tyke as he grew up. But Father
Gregoire was much too kind to bother anybody with this kind of
legalism and probably breathed a prayer as he poured the water
over the bald pate of this sniffling candidate that somehow the
boy would get on the calendar of saints some day and make
Vernon a saint's name. The probability of that happening was
akin to hoping that FDR would balance the budget from 1932
to 1945.

Besides if Father Gregoire had lived long enough he would
have seen the day when a whole raft of Holy Joes would get booted
off the calendar to make way for more ferials. Now ferials aren't
church janitors in Italy; they're ordinary weekdays, in liturgical
nomenclature.

Infant V. J. eventually got the wind coursing through his
lungs in good shape after that cold December day in 1919 when
he bowed into the post-World War I world and proceeded to
take a good hold on life. However, he didn't go through many
diaper changes in that bleak farmhouse sitting on that little knoll
in Cottonwood County. For only three months later, in March
1920, Pa bought a little 110-acre farm near Heron Lake. This
farm was known as the Schumacher Place, and the decision to
purchase this bit of real estate was one he lived to regret because, having paid too much for it in the short-lived boom following World War I, he soon lost it, and with it went all the
cash reserves he had to his name. This turn of fate guaranteed,
for one thing, that little V. J. was to grow up in the kind of
poverty which made St. Francis sing for joy and kept the little
fellow from becoming an unhappy playboy.

Perhaps a little family history is in order here. Pa was born and raised on the treeless prairies of north central South Dakota in the community of Hoven. One autumn when the crops weren't so good out there and there was no corn to pick, he journeyed to the Heron Lake area to husk the golden ears there and line his pockets with the coin of the realm which might serve to carry him throught the winter and enable him to purchase some seed in the spring for his quarter section in the land of the coyotes.

So, while squirreling around Heron Lake that fall, he met Ma somewhere, and she must have caused his eyebrows to quiver a bit because he pursued a courtship with this farm girl, Magdalen Knott by name, until he held hands with her in front of Father Matthias Jostock, on October 23, 1917, in the old frame church of Heron Lake.

He loaded his bride into his Model T Ford and clattered out to Hoven where they set up housekeeping on his farm north of town. However, Ma didn't take to the treeless habitat of the buffalo and longed for the cottonwoods by the Des Moines River back in Minnesota. She nagged Pa to carry her back to old Minnesota where she could watch the gophers disappear into their holes instead of listening to the prairie dogs bark all night.

Pa groused unhappily at the discontent of his wife in the land of Egypt but finally acceded to her wishes. He put the farm up for sale, and she, now heavy with child no. 1, was put on a train for Heron Lake in October 1918.

Gatherings his cows, horses, and some machinery, Pa chartered an "immigrant car," as they were called then, from the railroad and followed her back to the land flowing with milk and honey, traveling in the boxcar so he could minister to the needs of his livestock en route.

Uncle Ted, Ma's youngest brother, who had almost given up the ghost in a bout with pneumonia and had gone out to Hoven to recuperate for a spell, drove Pa's Model T back. This 1916 Tin Lizzie which I had occasion to gawk at and ride in as a wide-eyed little urchin later on, ran on kerosene and water and did it very efficiently too, according to Uncle Ted who took great interest in auto engineering at that stage in his life and gave testimony concerning this great Schaefer family chariot.

Later on, when Uncle Ted married and his household filled up with his progeny he took to preaching the Gospel to them as a sort of avocation, and some of the relatives opined that this was a carry-over from a desire he had once to become a priest.

Uncle Ted was great for telling stories of days past, and there was one I particularly enjoyed and which we will include here.

There was a large spread north of Heron Lake known as the Paul Farm. It consisted of over a thousand acres, used large machinery, and hired considerable help. Ted was hired one fall to man a ten-bottom plow pulled by a steam engine. Uncle Ted's job was to dance along the gang plank lifting up plows as they came to the end of the field and letting them back down again one by one as the rig moved back upfield. The rounds were two miles long each way, and Ted often lay down on the gang plank and snoozed on these long pulls. One afternoon, the engineer on the steamer also went to sleep. They both woke up when the steam engine altered its rhythm and pounded quite loudly. Too late. The rig was now already wallowing in the slough. Thirty horses couldn't budge the machine out of that quagmire. When winter set in they raised the machine by jacks anchored in the frozen mud and pulled it out. Uncle Ted was fired.

Upon the return of my immediate honorable ancestors to the promised land in October of 1918 they took up residence at the estate of Grandpa Joe Knott until dad could find a farm to buy and lose, and thus dissipate his material resources early in his married life. In the meantime, he farmed Grandpa's holdings there in Cottonwood County.

Soon after arrival back from Dakota, Alvina was born October 17, 1918, on this farm, and V. J., no. 2 of the clan, came along about fourteen months later. Alvina Rosella didn't like her name either and almost immediately became known as "Toots" in the family circle. The only time she wasn't called "Toots" was when Ma got mad at her for something. Then Ma addressed her as "Alveena" in a rather high-pitched voice.

CHAPTER II

Incident at "Chicken King's" Well

The Schumacher Place was a half mile north of Heron Lake, a block or so from Lakeside Cemetery, while the north boundary of the farm touched on the lake itself, Duck Lake. Duck Lake was rightly named, for in my youth it was a good breeding place for ducks. It was actually a big marsh full of bloated frogs and sorrowful sounding terns. In the spring the large volume of water in it gave it the appearance of a beautiful lake—for a week or two. The water level soon drained down to a couple of feet of stale green water in which grew tall marsh grass and cattails, except in the center, where the water level remained a little deeper and marsh grass grew not. Much of our youth was spent cavorting in one way or another around this big slough for at no time did we live more than a mile from it.

The Schumacher Place had a rather palatial home with a large front porch, and that's how one judged the elegance of homes in those days—by the size and extent of their front porches which, incidentally, were rarely used for anything. It was a large home, too, but before Ma and Pa could get a good start in filling it up with kids, they had to move. A big grove of tall cottonwood trees provided a windbreak for this house, a somewhat small hip-roof barn and a few other smaller outbuildings for the chickens and hogs. Across the country lane from this little farm was the city golf course where the more genteel members of society could exercise their flabby muscles.

Across the lane and adjacent to the golf course—actually directly across the road from the Schumacher Place—there dwelt a man on a tiny estate, a man who was known as "Chicken King." He came by that name because he eschewed a spouse and preferred to live with his chickens. Yes, he and his feathered friends occupied the same domicile. In addition, he cultivated a garden of sorts, pulled a few wormy apples off the trees in his tiny kingdom, and managed to keep body and soul together.

Chicken King was a short statured man, soft spoken, and quite philosophical in his observations. His wispy hair and beard were on the reddish side. His beard, which he allowed to grow a few inches below his chin, was sparse, but I can remember tugging at what little there was when I sat on his lap.

King was a close family friend for many years until he died. In addition, he was about the only babysitter Ma ever had, and he was also her chief adviser on the art of raising chickens, an activity which Ma had to pursue to provide most of the food and fabric for the Schaefer tribe.

King had an open well near his ramshackle two-room dwelling. To draw water from it he used the same method the Samaritan woman did in the Bible. He let down a bucket by a rope and drew up the full pail of water by pulling the rope across a pulley suspended from above.

In the New Testament there is a memorable scene at Jacob's well in Samaria when Christ got down to brass tacks with a Samaritan woman. In this journal we are about to depict a memorable scene at King's well. It was a rather traumatic experience for Ma although I was the one who should have been a bit more concerned with what transpired.

Alvina ("Toots"), going on three years old at the time, led me, a little chap of two, across the road to King's one afternoon of a quiet summer day. This was no unusual expedition for these two little Schaefers for we went over there quite often. For one thing we loved to listen to King cackle. Since he lived with chickens all the time his mode of speech was influenced a bit by them. For instance, his "koothchie-kooing" with little kids closely resembled the outpourings of a hen advertising her latest contribution to society in the form of a freshly laid egg. King wasn't home, however, this particular afternoon or he was catching some sack time on his pallet within his castle. At any rate, no adult was around to stop the questionable proceedings which followed.

Toots proceeded to hoist me into the bucket and let me down into the depths of the well where I bobbed around on the water inside the pail. I imagine sooner or later I must have become aware of my unusual environment and possibly deduced it wasn't very healthy and expressed increased displeasure with the situation by making like a banshee. Whether that attracted Ma's attention or she happened to be trailing her offspring that afternoon she never clarified. Eventually, she became apprised of the fact that no. 1 son was down in Chicken King's well and swiftly moved to extract him from said depths. Upon completing the rescue she undoubtedly proceeded to chastise Toots and post King's kingdom off limits for us two thereafter.

Later I read in the Bible that Joseph was put down into a well by his brothers and sold into Egypt. So I had one thing in common with this great Biblical figure even though I didn't become a big shot like Joseph and failed to figure very prominently in the designs of the Lord concerning salvation history.

While we were still residing on the Schumacher Place another member of the Schaefer tribe arrived. This was Marjorie Ursaline born on March 11, 1921. So it was evident that Ma wasn't pacticing birth control, the big "virtue" of the sixties, and it looks like it's going to be worse in the seventies for a new human being to sneak into the world. But poor Ma, she never spaced her children but let the Lord do it and had five in a row. According to the modern experts she should have collapsed physically and mentally. Approaching eighty now, she is as healthy as a horse. On the other hand, some of our modern mothers are killing themselves with drugs, gadgets, and worry lest they give birth to another child and are about as happy as a mouse eyeing an oncoming cat.

The year of grace given to redeem the Schumacher Place was up on March 1st, 1923, and we moved to the Hartneck Place a mile west down the road. By not paying interest for a couple of years Pa managed to scrape up a down payment on this ten acre farm. It consisted of a small bungalow type house, a little barn and garage combination, a hen house, tiny hog house, and a granary of sorts. You could raise lots of tomatoes in a garden and pasture a few cows, but that's about it. Pa had to scout around for additional land, and he found a quarter section which was half under water a good share of the time since Jack Creek cut through it. This piece of ground he rented from an absentee landlord was four miles south on the other side of the village. On the Hartneck Place we grew and waxed strong, but not strong enough to push over a horse. At the age of five we got mad at a sorrel we had, and one afternoon toddled out to the pasture where the animal was peacefully grazing, took a run at it and tried to upset the creature. That's how we got some sense knocked into our head at the tender age of five. Ma was trying to do the same thing with a razor strap, but the horse knocked us clear out and left a deeper impression in our rear end.

We grew to love the sound of the mourning dove in spring, climbing apple trees in the small orchard by the house, and watching Pa push the lawn mower, but most of all, we loved to ride in the old Model T Ford. We'll talk some more about that contraption later.

CHAPTER III

The Knott Place

At this point we might introduce the siblings who had the privilege of growing up with me and the place on which we grew up to be upstanding citizens of the Republic.

Alvina Rosella we have already met. She was the firstborn of the tribe and the one who lowered me into King's well, you remember. I was no. 2. Marjorie Ursaline, born on the Schumacher Place March 11, 1921, was no. 3. She was followed by Edgar Jerome on February 7, 1923. He joined the sacerdotal ranks with me after he cruised around a bit in the cruel old world and concluded his elder brother was having a nice go of it with a minimum of static. On November 22, 1924, Magdalen LaVera came into the world when we were living on the Hartneck Place. I remember the cries of tribulation emanating from the bedroom when "Maggie" was ushered into the world. None of us us was born in a hospital except the very late arrival, Darlene Mae Elizabeth, who joined our noisy ranks on November 6, 1936, when most of us were in high school.

One thing we all had in common was uncommon names, and none of us were too happy with the nomenclature fastened on us for life. Darlene was the name picked by the girls in the family for the belated arrival, and I thought that name smelled too. But names to the contrary, we weren't a bad looking crew as human mortals go.

We mention Grandpa Knott's demise elsewhere. Grandma Knott followed her spouse into the land beyond the sunset nine months later. I happened to sneak into the bedroom and watch the proceedings when she departed this valley of tears, and she seemed to make the transition peacefully enough. Both Grandpa and Grandma Schaefer accomplished their departures way out on the plains of South Dakota, and we weren't on hand to assist them in any way.

The Knott Place on which we spent most of our youth was adjacent to the Hartneck Place and became vacant when our Knott honorable ancestors died so we moved over there and occupied it for the time being. This "time being" lasted some thirteen years.

We didn't move from a small truck garden to a mighty ranch either. While the Hartneck Place comprised nine acres, the Knott Place consisted of only fifteen. Like the Hartneck complex, it consisted of a house and a few small outbuildings.

Back beyond the trees clustering about the house and yard area was a small barn which could accommodate six cows and two horses. Above it was a small haymow into which was pitched a load of hay by hand on occasion. Although the Sisters in school put out a rather vivid account of what hell was like, it was in that haymow one day that we experienced hell first hand as we were ordered to pull the hay back when it was pitched in through that small door on a hot July day. With no semblance of a breeze, the heat-charged air was filled with choking dust to the point of almost suffocating this freely perspiring little saint in overalls. The suffering son of Adam could think of only one thing—hell—and he vowed he would never commit a mortal sin and take a chance of having to endure this for eternity. Rural life in the old days had moments admirably geared to inculcating real sanctity.

Adjacent to the barn and forming the base of a T was the decrepit hoghouse. Here during the years of Depression, Dad valiantly strove to improve the status of the family exchequer by fattening a hundred or so pigs only to receive three or four cents a pound for the sleek Hampshires. This long low building had doors scarcely four feet high, and on occasion when trying to ride young calves in the hog yard, we had to dismount hastily when the incipient bovines headed pell-mell for one of these doors. A modern rodeo offers no charms to a farm lad who experienced those thrills personally before he was twelve. It was behind this shack that dad one day executed one of my favorite dogs with a shotgun because the canine had been caught eating eggs, a capital offense when eggs were worth a penny apiece and pennies were hard to come by.

On the south side of the agri-business courtyard stood the granary, the garret of which was used to house cluck hens in the spring while they patiently sat on eggs to form a new generation of egg producers. A lean-to off the granary provided a shelter for the family automobile as well as a catch-all for assorted junk and tools which had no set place but which caused Pa to bellow like a bull if one was found missing. Here, too, was the family arsenal which consisted of a rusting old twelve-gauge shotgun and a few moldy shells. The only time the blunderbuss was used was to execute dogs or cats guilty of eating eggs. On one memorable day when we were scarcely twelve years old we tried to execute a tomcat with said cannon only to be knocked down by the tremendous kick of the weapon. I suspect we will detail that frustrating scene later.

On the north side of the courtyard stood the hen house, a long, low, slant-roofed building constructed by orange hollow tile manufactured by the Heron Lake Brick and Tile Co. south of town, a firm which went broke even before the Depression. This building was extremely damp in the winter and caused much respiratory disease among the hens, the treatment of which consisted of smoking them with medicated vapor rising from a smudge pot. To leave a cozy house on a winter's night and have to go out to "smoke" chickens wasn't my idea of practicing medicine. The unfortunate part of it was that it didn't stop me from taking up smoking later in life, a habit I'm finding it very difficult to eradicate now.

Under a short row of box elder trees along the south side of the courtyard stood pieces of junk once serviceable as farm machinery.

The house wasn't too bad. It had a floor furnace, considered "modern" in those days; that is, the furnace was in the basement, and its register was flush with the floor and located as near the center of the house as possible to push heat toward all rooms. There wasn't any advantage to that arrangement except the dirty furnace didn't take up space anywhere in the living area. And then, too, when you got an earache all you had to do was lie on the floor over the heat register hoping the heat bathing the noodle might bring relief to the paining ear. This was Ma's idea of earache therapy, but it never dawned on her who was a Puritan like most everybody else in those days, that a laddie lying on the floor like that could peek under the dresses of the females parading by. Above the dining room where the furnace register was located was a small ceiling register through which heat could feed into the bedroom directly above. As a heat conductor, it was very inefficient, and served better as part of the intercom system. This bedroom was used by the girls in the family, and to find out from Ma what dress they should wear for this or that occasion, all they had to do was to put themselves on the floor and yell through the register to Ma, usually in the kitchen below.

The family indoor plumbing consisted of a pump over the sink which drew soft water from the cistern, but it always had to be primed first and was very noisy. Above the pump hung the razor strap which served two purposes, one of which, of course, was to instill a sense of law and order among the growing savages of the household. We found it much more pleasant when Pa used it to stroke his straight edged razor preparatory to removing a week's growth of coal black beard on Saturday nights. Despite Ma's constant nagging, he rarely ever shaved except on Saturday nights.

Probably the most important appliance in the house was the cook stove or range, used for everything requiring the application of heat—from cooking sweet corn to boiling water preparatory to butchering a hog. In charge of constantly refueling this cast iron calorific contraption was I, with the help of Edgar, who, when we carted in split wood every day to the woodbox by the stove, were often greeted by a sharp crack on the skull from the end of a broomstick. The girls, who were responsible for floor maintenance, looked with dismay on anybody tracking mud across a freshly scrubbed floor.

The house was one of those, common enough in that period,

which were characterized by the phrase, "six rooms and a path."
The path led out to a small slender building known by many
different names but which we shall call the "Center for Sears
Roebuck Research." Adjacent to that meditation parlor was the
woodshed back there in the grove. Corncobs were more available for fuel than wood generally speaking, so this shack was
usually half full of cobs, and half of them were rotten because
the roof leaked and kept them wet. To keep us occupied and
out of mischief when there was naught else to do, we kiddies
were commissioned to take a bushel basket, go out to the hog
pen and pick up these remnants of daily hog fests. The woodshed was never used as the traditional scene for spanking in our
family. Ma did most of the razor strap work right there on the
scene of the crime unless she had to run around the yard to
catch us first, and there, whether it be in the orchard or by the
mailbox, proper discipline was duly administered.

Also in the grove beyond the woodshed was a narrow tile
structure of dull orange color like the hen house. This was the
smoke house. Besides using it for flavoring the protein, we often
used it as a pulpit. The hollow tile was open at the corners, and
it was easy to mount to the gently arching cement roof. On this
we stood and preached eloquently, or so we thought, to the
sparrows, woodpeckers, squirrels or whatever wildlife happened
to be occupying the area at the moment. Despite these efforts,
which made Demosthenes a famous orator, we're told, we gained
nothing from the practice, apparently. In fact, we became one of
the world's worst pulpit orators in the Church.

Back of the house, between it and the orchard, was a heavy
thicket overgrown with raspberry, chokecherry, and gooseberry
bushes. Like bears, we lunched heavily between meals on these
berries, mostly gooseberries. The chokecherries tasted awful, and
we let the birds have them. The birds took most of the most
delicious berry of them all, the raspberry. This left us the gooseberry and some currants. When green, they both were frightfully
sour. The gooseberry made you shudder from the scalp to the
toenails when it was green, but became quite palatable when it
turned blue, while the currant simply could not be consumed at

all until it became ripe and turned black. The hens were fond of laying eggs in this thicket because they hoped to be able to hatch them before prying humans confiscated them. Ma insisted we crawl around in there looking for eggs every day, and we spent more time sampling berries than gathering eggs. Also when herding cows along the ditches in the area when drought dried up the pasture, we had nothing much to do most of the time but explore the ditches for berry bushes, which were usually located in shady areas. When the apples started to ripen out in the orchard, we abandoned the berry bushes in favor of this more filling fruit.

CHAPTER IV

"The Field"

A fifteen-acre farm isn't likely to provide sufficient hay and fodder to sustain five or six cows, a hundred hogs, a couple hundred chickens, a few sheep now and then, and four horses. So Pa cast about and found a bare quarter section about three and a half miles south. For some fourteen years we rented this piece of real estate, which was known as "the field." It consisted of about eighty acres on dry ground, and the rest a flood plain for Jack Creek, which wound through it. Much of the flood plain was wild meadow; some was swamp area overgrown with thick willow and prolific weeds. We cut the meadows each year and stacked up the fruit of this plain, and in winter we hauled it home as needed. To traverse three and a half miles aboard a clattering hayrack in the bitter cold was not my idea of graceful living. To separate the base of operations from the source of supplies was not my idea of efficient farming either.

Jack Creek was a slow meandering stream of muddy water about ten feet wide. Along its banks grew thick willows, a few cottonwoods, and a wide variety of weeds which when blooming would drive a hay fever sufferer to suicide. The stream abounded in dirty looking bullheads which were quite edible and a delight to catch. If you grabbed them the wrong way to extricate the hook you could get the palm of your hand impaled with a sharp spike imbedded in the top fin. If it tapped an artery you would have a thin geyser of blood spurting upward like Old Faithful. When that happened to me the first time, I barked like a startled watchdog.

A heavy rain in the summer would cause flooding in the meadowlands, and then we'd roll up the trousers, grab a pitchfork and wade out to spear carp, but Ma wouldn't cook them.

In the fall, the meadows and "jungles," as we called them, along the creek abounded in pheasants, but everybody else shot them

even though the land was posted. In our family the use of fire-
arms was verboten except to execute dogs and cats who ate eggs.
Pa built a small pole barn somewhere near the center of the
estate. It was used primarily as a site for harnessing and unhar-
nessing horses, a job which I detested and at which I was very
inept.

To provide water for the horses, Pa dug a shallow well which
produced about the worst tasting water to emerge from the
earth's gizzard and would quickly induce diarrhea in a wooden
Indian. It didn't seem to bother the horses, though. A small
hand-operated pump like the one above the sink at home dis-
gorged the stinking liquid only if you pumped it furiously.

The pole barn was encased with rough planks nailed about
an inch apart. When a windstorm came up and tore other buildings in the neighborhood to shreds, the old shack stood intact
because the wind could blow through it. By the barn a row of
decrepit farm machinery rusted peacefully in the sun. When we
had to use some of it, it would break down often enough in the
field, but it could be put back into service again by means of a
pair of pliers and some baling wire.

Until 1936 we farmed entirely with horses. Ma was adamant
against tractors. She thought they cost too much for what they
did in the field. Pa felt otherwise and did buy a couple of cheap
tractors. The first was a Fordson which wouldn't start, and when
it did, would overheat and blow steam around. The second was
a Sampson which was similar in looks to a Fordson but a little
heavier. On the first trip to the field with it, Pa hooked it up to
a quackdigger which required considerable horsepower. About
the second round the Sampson blew a rod clear out of the block.
Pa was so disgusted with it, he let it sit where it stopped and
for two years farmed around it. Finally, in 1936 he bought a new
John Deere Model B which we simply couldn't wear out.

In the meantime, we had four horses, faithful old animals,
but plugs of the first water. I doubt if any were capable of
galloping. There was Tom, Queen, Nellie, Nancy, and when the
latter died, there was Prince. Tom was the laziest of the lot and
fat. Queen and Nellie worked hard. Nancy, the youngest, worked

faithfully until she developed an ulcer in her belly and had to be shot. Prince, a light colored bay who replaced her, was a stalwart horse used to some speed and alacrity in the harness, but he soon lost his ambition when teamed up with our other plugs. Still, we always got the farm work done with these candidates for the glue factory.

One day Pa bought a team of fast broncos from some itinerant gypsies who roamed the countryside reaming the farmers. These two were a joy to drive when they weren't indulging in their bad habit of kicking over the whiffletree or going on a runaway expedition after being stung by bees in the hayfield. Pa had to get rid of them after they wrecked too much machinery and often had to be retrieved from some nearby county.

Many people today make a hobby of breeding horses and bouncing around on their backs in the saddle. Not for me. They never drove old plugs on the farm hour after hour. Horses simply lost their charm for me.

Now that we have established the setting, the time and the place, let's take a peek here and there at life on the land in the late Twenties and the Thirties.

School Days

CHAPTER V

The School Which Wouldn't Burn Down

When it came time for me to embark upon my academic career, I was carted up to an ancient frame structure in the village of Heron Lake and thrust into the hands of the Sisters who would attempt to inculcate the ABCs and some tidbits on how to go to heaven into my noggin. For this was a Catholic parochial school, and anyone in the Sacred Heart parish who didn't want to be regarded as a heathen and a publican, sent their offspring there and painfully extracted a dollar or two from the family exchequer to finance its operation when the long handled collection basket was thrust under their noses on Sundays. This sum was also supposed to cover the other expenses of running the parish in addition to operating the school. And just to heat that imposing baroque church whose twin towers dominated the village skyline was no small item. The pastor bought coal by carload lot and appealed to the husky men of the congregation to come in and help unload it.

Sacred Heart School wasn't anything to cheer about regarding its physical plant. It was a square clapboard building of ancient vintage. It had narrow high windows, a standard belfry tower found on so many small churches and schools in the late 19th century. It had been used for many decades as a public school before the good people of Sacred Heart parish latched on to it, placed a crucifix in each classroom and installed the well-swathed women of the Congregation of St. Francis of Our Lady of Lourdes as teachers to raise up new generations of scruffy kids in the love and fear of God.

The tall building housed four classrooms, some hallways, a creaking, well worn wooden staircase, and a partial basement where an old, worn out steam boiler hissed uncertainly and often enough hissed not at all—leaving the high-ceilinged rooms upstairs cold and cheerless.

A convent had been hung on to the rear of this venerable structure to house the dedicated women who labored so faithfully and so long, and who died and went to heaven. They have been accused of taking over too much of the religious instruction of children, leaving the parents free of that burden entirely. However, my observations were that parents preached plenty around the house, considerably supplementing the Sisters.

Every time Father Matthias Jostock, the energetic and industrious pastor of Bavarian stock, looked at that old school it gave him a pain in his medulla oblongata. He had constructed the most beautiful and one of the largest temples of worship in the diocese there at Heron Lake in that era, and he couldn't abide that old shack of a school to be considered a part of his empire. Still, the flock over which he harangued on Sundays would look darkly on paying for another new building for some years to come. They felt the debt on the church was squeezing them enough, but I have yet to hear of a Catholic who suffered very much because of what he gave to the church.

It was whispered about that the pastor prayed long and hard that God would send down a bolt of lightning to burn down the old school so he might collect the insurance and proceed to build a new one. The Lord didn't seem to oblige so the pastor could only hope that the building would catch fire from other natural causes. The question presented itself: How to get flames to flicker brightly over the old building without arson? A possible solution presented itself one day when the roof of the old building did ignite. It came about this way. Hedrick, the old janitor, had fired up the boiler with greater enthusiasm than usual on this particular winter's day, and sparks from the defective chimney settled on the nearby sloping roof, igniting the dry shingles.

The fire occurred in broad daylight, was immediately spotted, and the fire department took great delight in extinguishing it. However, I doubt if Father Jostock was so terribly delighted at the zeal of the fire lads.

As I understand, the fire chief counseled Father Jostock to rebuild the chimney to eliminate the fire hazard. And Father

Jostock no doubt affirmed his desire to do just that while in his heart he vowed that it would never be done and thanked God for answering his prayers in a rather indirect way.

The only problem left for the pastor was to get the fire drills perfected so that there would be no danger to the little lambs when the roof of the sheepfold started blazing. And how we drilled and drilled!

By and by, another blaze sprang up on that portion of the roof just before school was to start one morning. The fire department leaped into action, put it out quickly, and the pastor grunted with deep dismay over his doughnuts and coffee in the rectory. We kiddies growled also in deep dismay because the Sister would not allow us to watch the firemen put out the little blaze and instead marched us over to church on schedule to say the rosary. That's the closest I've ever came to renouncing my faith and quitting the Church.

Father Jostock's only hope now lay in the possibility of that same fire starting in the dead of night when the firemen were sound asleep and thus the fire could get a good start. One night the old Model T fire truck did come charging up to the school after the fire whistle moaned on and on for a long time in an attempt to rouse the protectors of villaged property. The pastor looked out of the window and couldn't see a wisp of smoke anywhere and again felt like kicking the lads, each and every one, in the seat of his pants. It was reported that a male resident of the village was trying to find his way homeward (whether he was in a state of inebriation or not has not been clarified); as he walked along he spied the red sanctuary lamp through the upstairs window of the convent chapel and thought the place was on fire.

Since Hedrick never fired up the boiler at night there was no chance of getting that old chimney to belch sparks then either, so a night fire was out of the question, and a night fire would be the only way to get the bastion in ashes. Father Jostock lost hope.

One year at about 8 A.M. on Holy Saturday I was on for serving the frightfully long ritual prescribed for that day. We were still bogged down in the vestibule blessing the new fire, the Easter candle, etc., when the fire siren (we always called it the "fire whistle") started to moan and scream and created a bit of excitement in the village as fire whistles do. Pauline Hager and Sienna Winkler, telephone operators in the exchange up over the bank, used to dread to hear that old siren because their boards would be jammed with calls from curious housewives inquiring where the fire was.

Now we were in the midst of performing the holy liturgy, and we couldn't interrupt it to step out the door and look for smoke although I was dying to do just that. I was more interested in watching the old Model T fire truck come clattering down the street. No sooner was I lost in my desires to abandon the sacred fire in front of me and go after a possible big one when Fr. J., without a pause in his Latin monologue, grunted to me, "Look outside and see if it's that doggone school again." I peeked out the door, taking my time about it, and saw the firemen ascend to the roof of Sacred Heart School to extinguish a small roof fire in the same spot where sparks had ignited shingles before.

I crept back into the vestibule and murmured, "Yes, Father, it's the school again." "Good," he replied, "I hope it burns down this time." But he knew it wouldn't. I think he had given up hope by now.

Then he told me to go into the sacristy and get him a cope. The Holy Saturday liturgy of those days required a change of copes—from purple to white and vice versa, and Sister must have forgotten to put a white one out there in the vestibule. I buzzed off without the forggiest idea of what a cope was and came trotting back with a stole since that was the best guess I figured I could come up with. The Padre was in bad enough humor because he lost another chance to get his school burned down and besides he was impatient with servers who goofed. The up-shot was that I got my ears pulled again. I have long ears now because they were stretched so often when I was a kid.

My first days in school were unhappy ones. I was shy and antisocial, stood around withdrawn and with stooped shoulders. That got me the nickname of "Bushy," named after Frank Bush, from the other kids. Frank was a bachelor who had a spinal ailment which caused him to walk around bent over, and he was given to growling at children, so they pestered the poor fellow cruelly. And that's the way they pestered me too until I finally shed the shyness and joined the human race. But you don't shed nicknames so easily, and I carried the damned thing almost clear through grade school.

Sister Ruth presided over the first and second grades, and I never ever made her wish that she had married the local drayman and never seen a convent or a convent school. I was a good boy. The naughty ones would have to shuffle up to the front of the room, hold out the palms of their hands, and she'd bring the ruler down sharply on said paws which, needless to say, were almost always quickly withdrawn when she raised the ruler so she had to grasp the fingertips of the victim to ensure that the target area wouldn't disappear.

My younger brother, Edgar, and the neighbor lad, Leonard Liepold, both given to considerable giggling in the first years of their academic training, were subject to the ruler treatment quite frequently, but to no avail. They giggled themselves out of a whole grade in school, that is, they flunked it and had to repeat it.

Sister Ruth, Lord rest her soul, was tall and slim and exhibited a placid smile most of the time from beneath her veil. She was holy and dedicated and manifested a great love for the missions. In fact, she often interrupted the academic flow for a "commercial" in behalf of the missions, and once or twice a week she sponsored mission marches. She'd set up the mite box on her desk in front of the room, and the kiddies who had begged, borrowed, or stolen a penny would march up to the receptacle and slip the coin into it with as much flourish as their phariseeism dictated. The practice made a crook out of me because I rarely had a penny clutched in my hot little hand, but I would march up there anyway with the rest and make the motions of popping one in the box just to win a smile from good old Sister Ruth. One of these days I should get around to doing penance for that and all the sins of my past life.

CHAPTER VI

The Syndicate

In the seventh and eighth grades there were some big boys who operated an extortion racket. These big bullies demanded that we timorous little runts journey down to the emporium during noon hour and buy them a penny's worth of candy or they'd beat up on us. Most of the time we didn't have a penny, and when we did we much preferred the jelly beans for our own consumption as we hoofed it home from school. I tried stalling them off as long as possible, but sooner or later the day of retribution came, and I got roughed up a bit under the bridal wreath bushes so Sister couldn't see what was going on.

One day when I had failed to deliver the "protection candy" I found myself flat on my back under the bushes and receiving ill treatment at the hands of one of the hoods when all of a sudden Father Jostock's swarthy hand reached in and grabbed my assailant by the scruff of the neck and proceeded to administer to him a thrashing which the incipient Al Capone must have remembered for a whole month. I forgot all the ear pullings in the sacristy, and Father J. became my hero, and maybe the incident helped spawn a vocation to the priesthood.

It wasn't exactly a one-sided persecution, however. I had a weapon available to fight back with, which those crude hombres were not aware of until V. J. sprung it on them suddenly one afternoon. On this particular day in the spring of the year when we had failed to deliver the candy, the bell rang ending the noon hour before the hoods could express their displeasure in their usual unpleasant manner, but little Vernie was solemnly warned that after school he'd get the deferred "treatment."

Three of these young bucks, walked home from school like me every day when the weather wasn't too fierce. The only trouble was they used the same route, and anywhere along the mile from the holy institution of learning and my domicile, their vengeance could be wreaked upon their recalcitrant little victim. To escape their clutches this enterprising little runt tore out of school after final prayer like a bolt out of the blue and hotfooted it home panting like a fox in front of snowmobiles. My dog, Boots, was waiting for me as usual. I collared him and dragged him to the bridal wreath bushes by the road, and when the toughs came loping along, I sicced Boots on them. Boots delighted in a commission like this, but he limited his activities to only extracting fabric from the legs or seat of the pants of his victims. So, a couple of them arrived home with some tears in their trousers to explain. The next day they solemnly warned me to keep my dog in the yard lest he "be blasted by a shotgun," and we gently reminded them that for every beating we received hereafter they could expect another assault from Boots. And that, my friends, was the end of the protection racket, as far as I was concerned, anyway, and I continued to grow up gaining wisdom and fearing God.

CHAPTER VII

En Route to School

En route to school we trod the gravel county road for about a mile. We lived at the edge of the city limits, and most of the route passed small five to ten acre farmsteads, "petite" farms maybe because the outbuildings were usually on a smaller scale than those out on the big country spreads. There was Ole Lundberg's across the road. Ole ran a milk route downtown and often we supplied him with additional milk from our herd when his own cows were slowing down too much to meet the customer demands. Then there was Fred Wille, John Tollefson (he had lots of chicken houses on his place), William Newcomer, the Nusser Place, and the Johnson Place, which we owned but rented to the Abernathys. Around a gentle curve, past the Liepold slough land, was the edge of the village proper. The first commercial business establishment we passed was the FitzHenry blacksmith shop, a fascinating place for little kiddies to poke their noses into, or, more likely, to stand at the door and look inside.

A block further was the railroad station of the Chicago Northwestern, Omaha branch. Painted a dark red, it was the typical railroad station house of that era. A low building with an overhanging roof sheltering the platform area which was paved with red brick and on which stood a few four-wheeled freight carts, loaded with cream cans mostly. When the next "passenger" came through, these cans would be stowed into the express cars to be taken to Lakeville or some other large creamery up the route toward the Twin Cities. For quite some time we shipped our cream to the Lakeville Creamery via the train.

As we thumped rapidly along to school in the mornings with no time to spare, occasionally a switching freight train might block our passage temporarily. This delay would most likely make us tardy for school, and we would have to stay after school to make it up, a prospect nobody enjoyed. Alvina, my sister, dreaded these confrontations with Sister which arose when we were tardy, and one morning she simply crawled under a freight car blocking the road and pushed on. I contemplated a like procedure, but while I debated the move, the train moved and eliminated further study of the question. Sister never found out about Alvina's passage through the Red Sea, but Ma did—one of us must have let it slip out—and there was weeping and gnashing of teeth. Ma gnashed the teeth and Toots (Alvina) did the weeping after the razor strap was put into action.

One morning in early spring when we had time to spare, for a change, on the way to school, we saw a little ruffian of the village come running out of the freight house section of the station. He galloped up to us and gushed excitedly, "You wanna see a man with his head cut off?"

No, I wasn't terribly anxious to view the phenomenon. Watching Pa stick pigs in the throat with a butcher knife didn't send me much, and a man deprived of his head would not add much to my day. Besides I didn't like the chap who bore the news. He got the best of me in fist fights several times, since I was not well trained in the manly art of self defense, and I unloaded some blood from my proboscis. Toots and Marge weren't interested either in gazing on somebody's severed neck. However, we made enquiry how it was that a man without a head was depostied in the freight shed of the Omaha depot. The little gangster didn't seem to care much about the history of the case, but gleefully held up a half dollar coin which he had filched from the dead man's pockets. Now we liked him less than ever. I always thought the chap would some day occupy the chair of applied electricity at one of our state institutions, but he turned out rather well after all. He's now raising a family and making an honest living, I understand.

As for how the poor mortal lost his head and was carried to the freight house, the matter was explained by the following issue of the **Heron Lake News**. He was a "bum," as we called railroad free riders, had been riding on the top of a freight car, lost his balance, and fell under the wheels. Sister led a prayer for the repose of his soul before class that afternoon, and the same afternoon he was buried in our Lakeside Cemetery at county expense.

The only other place en route to or from school which captured our attention much was the Davis & Hager store. It was here we lugged our eggs every week to be traded for foodstuffs and condiments we were not able to raise in the garden, and it was here that you could get a fair volume of jelly beans for a penny. Our honorable ancestors did not dole out pennies for candy—ever. However, Hedrick, the janitor at the school, found it necessary to clean out ashes from around the furnace once in a while or this piled up waste matter would seriously obstruct his maneuvering around the boiler. Whereupon he would recruit workers from the student body to haul ashes for a penny a day —a day being the length of the noon hour. When I heard the gospel story for the first time about the master of the vineyard hiring workers for the day and then paying them a penny, as the translation had it then, I thought to myself that the wages hadn't gone up much through the years. So, occasionally, with a penny pressed tightly in my dirty little hand, I was able to stop in at Davis & Hager to load up on a few jelly beans to sweeten up the hike home.

We didn't have to walk to school every morning of the year. In bad weather, if it was really bad, dad would take us in the car, the dirty old lumber wagon, or the sleigh in the dead of winter. Other times Otto Liepold might stop and pick us up since he ferried his boy, Leonard, to school almost every morning.

Otto, our neighbor to the north, got himself a brand new 1925 Model T sedan with four doors and big high windows. Shortly thereafter he accidentally tipped it over into his slough and got it all muddy. It was a shame to see that gleaming black car now defaced with mud and streaks of dirty water.

Eugene Liepold lived a half mile further north than Otto, and he too would extend an act of kindness and stop to pick up the scruffy Schaefer kids as he ferried his brood to the parochial institute of learning, praying, and rubber hosing, if you got too far out of line. Eugene had a new 1929 Chevrolet with a six-cylinder engine, a much lower profile than a Ford, and nice blue upholstery. Chevrolet was beginning to knock Ford around pretty badly because they sensed the people wanted style and luxury in their automobiles, and Chevy was beginning to stick a little of it into their low-priced car while Ford was all function and practicality, and for that the Model A of the period was a classic.

While Henry Ford wanted people to have a car which was good for them and economcial, the customers were beginning to demand some pizzazz and power, and the American automobile was to become a status symbol, a lethal missile, literally a mobile coffin.

As we arrived at the clapboard castle either by foot or by a "bummed" ride, other autos were in evidence disgorging their offspring, not many like you would find today, but a few who lived way out on the fertle prairie. One of these cars one couldn't fail to note because as it approached the school heavily loaded with humanity, its engine was turning out high rpm's. That could be none other than August Freking. August was a short stout man of German stock who sired nineteen kids and had almost a dozen of them going to school at the same time. He had a couple of these 1929 Chevrolets, insisted on driving one of them himself, but knew very little of the mystery of their gearboxes. I've never seen him drive in any gear but low, but the kids insisted that when he got out into the open countryside he managed to get it into high. However, if a six-cylinder engine was heard in town singing a fairly high note, it was August Freking driving in low gear around town, and only in low gear.

CHAPTER VIII

Ashes and Rubber Hose

When winter came in earnest it didn't make much difference if one walked to school or rode in an open sleigh. By the time we arrived, our red corpuscles were beginning to congeal. In each classroom were leaky and spitting steam radiators. We'd huddle over them to thaw out, and for the rest of the morning, the hissing and spitting of these radiators was music to our ears while the sound of the teacher's voice decidedly was not.

Occasionally, the radiators were silent and cold, which meant that the decrepit old boiler had broken down again. Or maybe Hedrick, the janitor, hadn't gotten around to cleaning out the ashes below the grates and the fire slowly suffocated. Father Jostock would get after him, and he would hire us poverty stricken urchins to haul it out during the noon hour. Sometimes he would pay as high as a penny a bushel. More likely a penny an hour. Francis Hughes and V. J. had as much to do with keeping the heating system of Sacred Heart School operating as anyone by their ash operations.

Hauling ashes also kept us out of some mischief. In the rear of the school building were two small buildings, one for the girls and one for the boys. Occasionally during the winter on balmy days there ensued during the noon hour what might be called "The Battle of the Backhouse." The big boys (same ones who beat me up when I didn't deliver the candy), noting when the fortresses were well populated with visitors, would commence with an incessant volley of snowballs which served to trap the visitors inside. This was a rather distressing situation for the girls, particularly, or sounded that way. Females, of course, tend to sound the siren for any little thing because they are more emotional. Sister Superior, noting the outcries from the outhouse, found it difficult to arrange a truce once the melee was in progress.

Whereupon she sent a little emissary over to the rectory to report on the civil war in progress out in the boondocks, intimating that a firm hand was needed to restore order, a hand a bit firmer than hers.

Father Jostock always looked darkly on this laying of unauthorized sieges on the institution's comfort stations—mostly because of the damage incurred to the buildings. Each building was fronted by a lath shield designed to add some privacy. Snowballs fractured these fragile pieces of wood very easily, and they cost some money, not much, to replace, but Father Jostock had no money for foolishness of any kind—ever.

Upon the receipt of the emissary's message, Father came bolting from the rectory, collared a few culprits, and there followed an exercise which was an essential part of the curriculum, namely the pounding of posteriors with a stout rubber hose.

Today, one in authority dares not touch a scamp in dire need of a spanking. The punk, however, can shoot, stab, or mutilate the teacher however he desires and be fairly assured that he won't be punished for it. In those days there was no objection to the school authorities using corporal punishment on a child if, in their judgment, it was the advisable course of action to follow.

At Sacred Heart, the rubber hosing was reserved to the pastor because only he had sufficient energy and strength to administer it. And the thump of the hose being applied to the seat of the pants could be heard all over the building, and, among other things, it considerably dimmed the enthusiasm of the Sir Knights of the Snow Brigade to launch further sieges on fortresses in the rear of the castle.

When the blows sounded particularly sharp, we knew that a broad geography book had been inserted in the trousers by the victim for his own protection. However, a pause always ensued, while the armor was removed, and the thumps resumed. One of the wild hoods up in the seventh and eighth grade room fired an ink bottle at Sister one day, and his session in the "cage" was the longest we can remember. This "cage" was a sort of cubbyhole enclosure in the hallway upstairs. Originally designed,

I suspect, as a principal's office, it was never used for anything much except as a place wherein these quick courses in applied child psychology could be administered.

They didn't take Willie to a psychiatrist or a school psychologist to try to find out why he was always so naughty. They just tanned his hide, and sometimes Willie even turned out to be a priest.

CHAPTER IX

Landscaping and Liturgy

The Reverend Superintendent, Father Jostock, may have wielded the rubber hose when he had to in order to maintain discipline, but he generally was very pleasant and loved to tease the children. On sunny days sometimes he would show up on the playground during the noon hour, snatch the bonnets off the girls and parade around with one or two on his head, much to the mirth of the little girls, who squealed with glee.

With the arrival of spring, however, ther was no more playing around during the noon hour either for him or for us boys. He was a lover of natural beauty, had extensive flower beds scattered about on the church grounds and also in the village park which fronted the church. He became self-appointed curator of the village park since its beauty would enhance his stately baroque church.

Once spring arrived, he needed manpower in order to rake his kingdom in town plus the cemetery two miles north of the village. He solved that situation by putting the able-bodied boys of his school to work during the noon hour. When the bell rang signaling the end of the noon hour, he ignored it and kept us working. We didn't complain. Pushing a rake was still preferable to pushing a pencil. Sister didn't like it, but there wasn't a thing she could do about it. Sisters were obedient little handmaids in those days, meek and humble of heart. Some pastors took advantage of them and treated them rather poorly. However, with the coming of Vatican II, the holy maidens went on a revolution and wouldn't take any more guff from the male master in the rectory.

Father Jostock loved flowers and maintained flower beds all over the church property, thus enhancing the beauty of the stately structure. He had his plantings so timed that when one species would finish blooming, another would begin. He needed help with his flower beds, and Hedrick wasn't able to assist him much, so the 7th and 8th grade boys from his reform school were pressed into action.

I've often wondered why more churches don't do more toward beautifying their grounds. They may spend a half million for the building and its interior glorification, and maybe a hundred dollars for landscaping.

Father Jostock must have picked up his love of natural beauty in his native Bavaria, where the cultivation of flowers, we noticed on several trips, is part of their culture, it seems, and makes their countryside and villages the most beautiful in the world, I think.

As he was a promoter of natural beauty around and outside the temple, Father Jostock was also a promoter of liturgical beauty inside. He was great for processions on religious feasts, i.e., Christmas, Easter, Forty Hours Devotions, Holy Thursday, Palm Sunday, and Corpus Christi. As one of the servers, I spent many hours rehearsing, marching, swinging the censer, carrying candles, palms, crucifixes, and whatnot. We genuflected properly, folded hands correctly (making sure they were properly washed first—almost an impossibility for a growing boy), bowing, and sometimes sleeping during the sermon. The pastor wouldn't notice it because his back was to the servers when he was in the pulpit, but the people did, and there would be some sharp scolding after we got home.

When we weren't sleeping, we'd be gazing at one of the large stained glass windows facing us. It featured the sacrament of matrimony. The top panel showed Abraham and Sarah holding hands and cementing their nuptials in the presence of a rabbi. The lower one featured Mary and Joseph engaged in the same activity. After sitting on the bench in the sanctuary and studying these panels for years during sermons, we eschewed matrimony in favor of holy orders.

Enhancing the liturgy was the large pipe organ installed in the choir loft when the church was built, and still used to this day. This instrument required considerable maintenance over the years, but is still capable of sending sound cascading from the vaulted ceiling. At the close of religious festivals, Beatrice Meixner, the organist now for fifty years, pulled out all stops as the pastor led the congregation in singing "Grosser Gott" with great enthusiasm.

CHAPTER X

Grandpa Dies

I was five years old when I met death for the first time. Grandpa Knott, who lived on the next place south of our little farm, had died.

The last time I saw him alive he was sitting up in a chair in his living room, and a white sheet covered his legs. Ma told me to quit pestering him because he was sick. So I couldn't crawl up on his lap and tug at his bushy black beard which hung half way down to his chest. I was a terrible beard puller, they tell me, from the time I was two years old and used to sit on neighbor "Chicken King's" lap and work him over. He was a little man with a reddish wispy beard, and it was hard to get a handful of hair when working on him. If he had swatted me a few I might have quit pulling beards—and girls' hair later— but King was a very patient man with little kids.

The next thing I knew Ma was awful sad and said Grandpa Knott had died. That night she took us all over to Grandpa's house. There were a lot of people there, but I couldn't find Grandpa anywhere. Some of the other kids said he was out on the front porch, but nobody was supposed to go out there. This was an enclosed porch which was never heated in the wintertime, and it was mighty cold out there. (This was December 14, 1925.) I couldn't figure out why they put Grandpa out in such a cold place. I found out later on that embalming wasn't done very much in those days, and so they tried to keep dead people in cold storage, if possible, until the undertaker, Otto Burreau, a short heavy-set man with a bald head, arrived with the coffin, installed him in that, dolled him up a bit, and hauled him into the living room for the wake.

But I had to satisfy my curiosity about Grandpa and sneaked out to the front porch when nobody was looking. There he was sleeping on some planks supported by sawhorses and covered with a white sheet, but all I can remember was that I wasn't terribly thrilled to see one of my honorable ancestors resting in peace under a sheet, and I figured that Grandpa, who was such a nice man, deserved something better. But I certainly didn't suffer any trauma or acquire any fear of dead people. I protested to Pa about Grandpa freezing out there on the porch, and he wiggled his big finger at me and warned me if I went out there again I'd get whopped.

The next night Grandpa was in the warm living room and all primped up in a black coffin. Lots of people came trooping through to take a peek at him and murmur something about "how nice" he looked. Then they shook hands with Ma and the rest of the clan, sat down, and looked solemn.

Pretty soon the priest came barging in, and everybody mumbled the rosary real fast because they couldn't dig into the grub till that was done. I had to stay put in the corner until the commotion started with everybody eating, and then when nobody was watching me anymore, I crept to take a look at Grandpa sleeping so soundly in his coffin. I marveled how fancy his bed was with all those silken frills and such, but I figured as long as he was going to sleep a long time until the angels woke him up, like Ma said, he might as well be comfortable and have a fancy bed. But I couldn't figure out why he wanted to sleep in his best Sunday suit because people don't do that. So I hopped out to the kitchen and asked Ma about it, and she told me to scram. I went back and surveyed Grandpa some more and became more perplexed. I never saw anybody in bed with his hair combed, and his beard combed, too. In fact, Grandpa never combed his beard even when he was up. I hustled back to the kitchen to get that puzzle cleared up, and Ma stuffed some cake into my mouth and told me to go upstairs and play with the other kids.

Instead, I went over to where Louie Winkler was sitting because he was such a jolly man and liked to throw me up in the air. Sitting beside him was his wife, Mary, who was Ma's cousin. She was talking with another woman, and I could hear her say, "You mean he is just going to have a rough box? I'm going to have a vault 'cause I don't want any snakes coming around me."

Mary was always so terribly afraid of snakes, and when she saw one in her garden she wouldn't go out there again for a week. In the meantime, Louie would have to patrol it a half dozen times to make sure the snake had moved on.

However, I never forgot about those snakes prowling around cemeteries and for a long time I tried to find a snake hole over a grave, and never did find one. Later, one day Pa disgustedly tossed his shoulders and growled at Mary when she got on the subject again. "Ach, snakes don't burrow down that deep in the ground. Wassa matter witchya?" But that didn't convince Mary, and when she died, sure enough, she had the best vault money could buy.

I didn't get to the funeral because Ma said I couldn't sit still, but I watched Otto and the men load up Grandpa in a fancy gray hearse and head for town with everybody following in their Model Ts, Essexes, and Dodges. Then I went back into the kitchen to clean up some cake left over from the wake.

Such was my introduction to the phenomenon of death. And, as I say, it didn't bother me much. Ever since I have accepted it as a natural course of events for the poor human race as a result of Adam's sin.

CHAPTER XI

The "Corpse" Wasn't Dead

It was a winter evening in 1931. Minnesotans were shivering from a deep economic depression as well as from the cold weather. The neighbors had gathered at our humble farm home for a social evening of card playing. Neighborhood socials were more common then than they are now. Maybe they were trying to forget their economic troubles.

While their elders flipped the pasteboards across the bare tops of tables in the dining room, their offspring had to manfacture their own entertainment. The locale of this entertainment was often shifted upstairs by parental mandate to minimize the noise pollution created by the young.

On this particular night upstairs we decided to play "funeral." I, eleven years old, preempted the role of the priest because I was big enough to knock down anybody who contested my self-ordination. Vested in a blanket from one of the beds, I found an old arithmetic book to serve as a ritual, and I was ready for business. The coffin was a trunk which stood in the hallway. It was hastily emptied of folded bed linen and pillow cases. My brother, Edgar, eight, was selected to be the corpse, and he folded himself inside this improvised casket and was commanded to keep his eyes closed.

All (some dozen neighbor kids) put on long faces as they marched past the open "casket" and peered at the "corpse" as they had seen their elders do at wakes. The rosary was also recited but with one big change: Only one Hail Mary was recited between mysteries instead of ten. Children are very honest about making liturgical changes when the customs of their elders seem a bit tiresome to them.

Came time for the burial, the trunk was closed, and the pall-bearers struggled valiantly to get it to the edge of the stairwell (grave) where I assumed my position at the head of the stairs and began mumbling unintelligibly (like most priests did in those days) while peering into the arithmetic book and concluded the ritual by sprinkling the trunk with "holy water." The aspergill consisted simply of a piece of wood used to prop the window open in clement weather.

The trunk was let down into the grave with ropes made from rags tied together. They had been procured from a pile Ma had accumulated in the storeroom to make a quilt. However, at the strategic moment when the coffin was hanging in mid-air over the stairwell, one of the fragile ropes broke.

The coffin clattered down the steps, tore open the door at the bottom, and slid on its side into the dining room where the elders were playing cards. The "corpse" suddenly came back to life and screamed lustily until released from captivity.

Up above at the head of the "grave" the faces of the priest and the mourners froze in horror at the turn of events, and then recovering from their momentary paralysis, bolted to seek refuge in closets and under beds as irate elders invaded the "cemetery" to seek an explanation of this most unusual phenomenon.

I, now an ordained priest, recall that incident as my first "funeral." But instead of receiving a fee for it, I got my ears soundly boxed.

CHAPTER XII

The Time I Almost "Croaked"

Before I was old enough to misspell c-a-t I almost died and went to Heaven one day. I was six, maybe seven, when Ma trundled Toots and me down to get our tonsils out. In one epoch of medicine, physicians almost bled people to death in an attempt to cure them. In our age, "bleeding" was no longer done. But sometimes the patient bled to death anyway when the surgeon was trying to do something else. That's what almost happened to me.

When I was a kid the standard procedure seemed to be to dig down and get the tonsils out of every kid who ever got a sore throat or who even suffered a big wart on his knuckles.

Neither Toots or I manifested much enthusiasm for the proposed therapy for whatever was ailing us. She kicked, screamed, tore at Ma's dress every foot of the way from the car into the hospital. Lest she cause too much of a disturbance and alarm the suffering sinners incarcerated there, she was hauled immediately into the doctor's office where they put her away with a bottle of ether and then proceeded to deprive her of those two little appendages in her throat God must have made a mistake in putting there in the first place.

That left me sitting out in the waiting room and looking very forlorn. Up on the bookcase in the waiting room a skull stared at me from its empty eye sockets, and I was convinced that the poor chap had come in to have his tonsils out too and that's how he ended up. I became very depressed. Maybe I had a special revelation that within the next twenty-four hours I would be very close to the Pearly Gates.

When my turn came I was led into the execution chamber, hoisted up on the table, and soon gone on a fast merry-go-round into oblivion after the nurse laid a strip of gauze soaked in ether over my schnozzle.

55

The two nodules of mine were deep down in the throat, I was informed later, and the good old doc sliced up a little extraneous tissue down there in the attempt to filch out what he was after. That unloosed the floodgates later and also gave me a sore throat which perdured off and on for ten years.

The rest of the day in the hospital produced considerable discomfort for the little laddie. Then, as night approached, we were taken home.

It was during the night that the mangled throat began to leak blood again rather freely, and when the stomach had enough it erupted the red stuff in big gushes over the bedsheets. Ma crumpled into a dead faint when she beheld the crimson tide.

The doc was hauled back in on the scene at three o'clock in the morning out there to the farm to administer some chemicals designed to prevent any further waste of young V. J.'s already severely depleted lubricating oil.

Today I'm sure I'd have been taken back into the hospital, and a plastic tube would have been inserted into my pipelines somewhere to help replenish some of the drained liquid. I survived without that auxiliary power because maybe the Lord figured the little fellow might be of more use to Him if he were left on the globe for a bit longer.

CHAPTER XIII

High School Days

May 1933 arrived and signaled the end of eight years of training for us in the bosom of Holy Mother Church at Sacred Heart
School. At the completion of that month of May the parish
cheerfully unloaded some eight financial liabilities who had completed the eighth grade. Among them was my sister, Alvina
(Toots) and myself.

There wasn't any graduation ceremony, even though completing the eighth grade was something of an accomplishment,
since not every kid went on to high school in those days. A few
of the boys, some of whom weren't too excited about academics
in the first place, were now permanently shifted to plows, manure
spreaders, and milk stools by the agricultural barons who ruled
their households. A high school education was still considered
somewhat of a luxury by some when muscle power was needed
to block off the wolf nipping at the doorposts during the Great
Depression. At any rate, high school, then as now, was for some
just a period of loafing and infantile romancing. I suspect there
are more kids leaving high school today who can't read than
there were in our time. High school commencements today are
so meaningless that I don't attend them unless I have to invoke
the name of the Lord as a clergyman of the community.

We ended our grade school days with an outing to Mankato
Good Counsel Academy. For the lower classes the year ended with
a picnic somewhere nearby, and we had picnicked our way
through a half dozen grades by now during the lovely month of
May. Now we were to experience a real outing for a change.

But first let's look at an average year-end school picnic. The
Sisters would conscript a couple of adults to assist in shepherding
the flock into a strange pasture for this event. We were usually
marched across the Omaha railroad tracks to the shore of Duck
Lake beyond. Here we could spend a few hours chasing each

other around the gooseberry bushes, and after some of that type of exercise, we wolfed a sandwich provided by a committee of mothers. Committees of mothers in small communities accomplish a lot in the way of practical needs but usually aren't given much credit for anything. The climax of the outing was the serving of one ice cream cone to each little peasant. Ice cream cones were considered a great delicacy, and poor kids got a chance to wrap their tongues around them only on the occasion of a Fourth of July picnic or maybe during a summer band concert if the paterfamilias felt disposed to shell out a nickel to his gasping offspring.

Duck Lake wasn't considered a plush picnic spot by anybody because of its murky water from which sprung acres of long waving cattails. Its muskrat colonies didn't lend an aura of pastoral beauty to the scene either. But it was but a short march from Sacred Heart School, and when you try to march a motley group of urchins zipping five directions at once, you have to limit the expedition to a short route.

However, it did have a grove of trees on its sloping banks, and a few patches of grass here and there, kept cropped by some farmer's roving bands of bovines who left a few "cowpies" around as marks of their passing while ingesting the bluegrass. In our small world, the banks of this overgrown slough appeared as romantic as the environs of Loch Lomond we had read about in Sir Walter Scott.

For our completion of the eighth grade, however, the Notre Dame nuns who had replaced the Franciscans when we were in the seventh grade had something more grandiose in mind. Apparently, they wanted to make a last ditch stand for vocations among the girls who would soon be released into the cruel but captivating pagan world of a public high school. No doubt they had singled out two or three of these unsuspecting girls to don the coif. A trip to their citadel on the hill and their nursery of nuns up there on Good Counsel, they must have reasoned, might serve to solidify the multitude of hints they had been casting at their female charges all year.

I doubt if those holy nuns were worldly-wise enough to fathom the extent of the pull exerted on these girls already by the members of the male sex, but they suspected it, I'm sure. At any rate, the Holy Spirit must be given a chance to exert an opposite pull by a visit to the hallowed halls of the Motherhouse.

We boys in the class were taken long for the ride and because we would howl too much if we were left at home. After all, a ride to Mankato was a considerable expedition for most of us who had not been beyond a twenty mile radius of our prosaic little village of Heron Lake.

For the trip to Mankato, Mr. Peter Oster who lived across the street from the school in his bachelor apartment and who peddled Raleigh products, furnished his Buick, and Mildred Haas, who taught in a country school somewhere in the area, furnished her Chevrolet. We boys piled in with Mr. Oster while the girls and Sister went with Mildred.

Peter was a kindly old gent, a bit on the heavy side. His greying hair protruded out from a floppy hat, and a pair of worn suspenders kept his baggy pants up. He furnished free cough medicine for the Sisters and transportation whenever they needed it, which wasn't often, because Sisters didn't ride with male drivers whenever they could avoid it in those days.

We boys were more impressed with riding in Peter Oster's Buick than with the Mankato Motherhouse. The Buick had a long hood sticking out in front and didn't rattle and howl at fifty miles an hour like our 1928 Dodge did.

Perhaps a visit to a girls' school should have been an exciting prospect for us boys, but we weren't sufficiently matured yet to see much charm in females. And then we didn't have sex thrown at us from morning till night through the media like the poor kids today. We were allowed to enjoy our youth and didn't have to grow up so fast like the kids today. Furthermore, with all the farm work to do, we were too busy to think about sex. As a matter of fact, when the Sisters made such a fuss with the girls because their petticoats were showing or if they didn't wear one at all, we couldn't figure out why they made such a big production out of it. The last thing we noted about girls was their petticoats. Or whether they wore makeup or not. Sister would call them "flirts" if they pasted their faces with something out of mother's jar.

However, in the year of Our Lord 1973, things are different. Girls troop to school half naked in miniskirts which are getting more and more mini, and I suppose the boys can't help gazing upon their bare thighs and suffering considerable distraction therefrom. In fact, it is not outside the realm of possibility to find a "Sister" wearing a miniskirt. When a nun goes "nuts" what can we expect of the kids? The poor things are assailed with so much temptation and false standards, it's a wonder they don't turn out to be sex fiends by the time they are fourteen. Statistics show all too many fall into the sex trap at tender ages, and have their youth wrecked by it. Stupid adults who cannot resist immodest fashions, nay, are slaves to fashion and corrupt mores are to blame.

Now faced with the harvest they sowed, some adults have the queer idea that sex education in the schools will cure sex run rampant among the youth. The only trouble is that such sex education lacks the most important ingredient of all, moral training, so it's worse than nothing. Conscientious parents will have to take up the task of giving sex education in the home and in the proper aura of reverence for this great gift of God.

As we intimated before we got into this sermon on sex, our interest revolved more around cars than girls when we graduated from the eighth grade—cars and tractors. Which brings up one of life's little tragedies for a young boy—how the family came so close to getting a new car but didn't.

It was a lovely Sunday morning in summer. After Mass Pa got his hands on a gleaming new black 1932 Chevrolet coach and came rolling up the driveway in it. We all took a ride in it, and the pressure was on the honorable progenitors to buy it— pressure from us kids who jumped and yelled all over the place with enthusiasm for this shiny hunk of machinery. Of course, the status of the family exchequer didn't figure at all into our adolescent mode of thinking. We had no idea of the Schaefer checkbook balance except that it might possibly be a bit inadequate, at least according to Ma's often expressed opinion. However, she somewhat reluctantly gave her consent to buy the chariot. Enthusiasm is contagious, I guess.

Pop went back to town to close the deal. But the dealer, Fred Freer, was out someplace or sleeping late, and the menial poking around the office could only assure Pa that Fred would get in touch with him as soon as he came in. When he gave Pa the keys to snort around in that demonstrator he had quoted its price, $585.00 which, of course, today we would consider to be "chicken feed."

But second thoughts concerning the project manifested themselves in the interim before Fred got wind of a badly needed sale of a new car and came bounding out to the Schaefer Chateau after dinner to close the deal. Had he been on the scene from the start, we undoubtedly would have had a new car, but because he wasn't around to strike while the iron was hot, he lost a sale despite hanging around for a couple of hours trying to persuade Pop to latch on to the new buggy. It turned out to be a sad day for us kids who had our hopes up so high only to end up casting contemptuous glances at the old Dodge and angrily kicking its tires.

The summer of 1933 passed quickly enough with its quota of toil and perspiration. And it wasn't with much enthusiasm that we plodded to the portals of Heron Lake High School for the first time that September to absorb some secondary education. The ancient three story fortress with its high ceilings and long narrow windows set amidst red brick and its belfry tower pointing into the sky looked like what we considered the state penitentiary to be. And now we were going to rub elbows for the first time with pagan kids (everybody not Catholic was considered more or less a pagan and as an enemy of righteous living). We felt a bit uncomfortable as we shuffled into this fortress for the first time that September morn.

But soon a bright spot appeared on the horizon within those forbidding looking walls. That bright spot was the principal, Miss Frances Johnson. She was a neat appearing young woman about five feet tall, with light brown hair which she usually wore gathered up into a pug in the back. Right off she smiled at me when I crept into the assembly hall for the first time and looked for my desk. From then on I always walked past her desk and greeted her as I came in every morning to begin another tiresome day among a motley group of kids none of whom I particularly cared much about. I guess I developed a bit of a crush on Miss Johnson, and my going out of my way to shyly bid her "Good morning, Miss Johnson" each day brought criticism from my peers who didn't like my attempt at a little "apple polishing."

Miss Johnson also taught English and endeared herself to me even more one day when I asked a somewhat stupid question: "Miss Johnson, what is a novel?" The class snickered because I guess everyone else knew what a novel was except me. Miss Johnson reprimanded the inconsiderate louts for making fun of little V. J. and very patiently explained to me what a novel was. Here I had been reading them by the dozens; in fact, all of the juveniles and the classics found in the library of creaking old Sacred Heart School, and didn't know what they were called.

Miss Dorothy Mortenson was a well proportioned brunette who taught algebra, and I liked her too. At first I didn't, because of one of the remarks she made to me one morning early in my high school career as I trooped into the brick shack. Like all teachers, she was standing guard in the halls as the lads and lassies stumbled and jostled toward their home rooms. She said to me as I sheepishly crept by her in the hall: "You have such cute curly hair." No lad at that age cares much about that kind of compliment. It's true I had a fair crop of light brown curly hair, and now I wish I could have retained it. Then and for the most part thereafter, it was rarely combed into any semblance of order nor washed often enough. Still it used to make females want to run their fingers through it. In the case of my mother, it was a convenient anchor for her fingers when she wanted to arrest my progress for the purpose of inflicting chastisement.

Miss Mortenson taught mathematics, and in that class I became interested in female legs for the first time as I gazed at her well proportioned limbs. But even that didn't make algebra very palatable. It was my weak subject, and I managed to avoid further courses of all mathematics even in college.

Miss Agnes Christenson taught Latin and history and did a tremendous job in the classroom. In fact, she was the most outstanding teacher I've ever had in the twenty years I was required to spend in classrooms in order to qualify for my august profession.

I don't know just why I signed up for Latin I, which she taught, as I wasn't dreaming about wearing my collar backwards at the time. It was a most fortunate stroke of fate in view of later developments that I took her Latin course. She gave us such a solid foundation in the language of the Caesars that, despite my lack of intellectual genius, I found future studies in that language comparatively easy. It was probably that daily drilling in the fundamentals of Latin grammar at the blackboard that did it. We were the ones who stood at the blackboard, not she, and we scratched away declensions and conjugations as she crisply commanded.

Miss Christenson was a tall dark-haired woman who was all business in the classroom and brought her pupils into a no-nonsense mood. Through her, via her history course, we were introduced to a figure by the name of Adolf Hitler who at that time was gobbling up considerable real estate in Europe. She issued dire warnings to watch this Schicklegruber, for he posed quite a threat to world peace, according to her. Up to then I had heard only praises about the Blackshirt from a kraut eater in the neighborhood who felt Hitler was God's gift to the oppressed Fatherland of his kinfolk who were having a sticky time of it ever since they bit off more than they could chew in World War I.

This was the beginning of deficit spending under President Roosevelt, a harbinger of things to come in mismanaging the wealth of the nation. One day Miss Christenson informed us that the U.S. was some three billion dollars in debt, and I had visions of the country going bankrupt. So did Pa. He listened faithfully to Father Charles E. Coughlin from Royal Oak, Michigan, every Sunday afternoon. This priest orator apparently had as much adulation for F. D. R. and his fiscal policies as he had for a skunk taking quarters under his church. The radio priest had many unpleasant things to say about international bankers, Jews, the Federal Reserve system, and our President. Pa lapped it all up and cussed in dismay.

I suspect now that Charles E. was hitting at that infernal outfit already in existence, the Council on Foreign Relations, the band of the rich and powerful who have designs on running the world and are now using Communism as a lever to further their ambitions.

Anyway, along with Pa I became an avid listener to Father Coughlin until one day his bishop told him to clam up, after he called F. D. R. some choice names which caused the White House to get on the bishop's back. And what do you know? The good priest obediently shut up. Imagine something like that happening today! With these rebels we've got in the Church today, we're in rather bad shape. Methinks the devil is having a bit of a fling in the sheepfold, and the barque of Peter has entered some mighty rough seas.

Now with the national debt over 400 billions, I've ceased to worry too much about temporalities like that, and chosen to concentrate more on people going to hell, as is more fitting to one in the role of a shepherd.

Also on the faculty was a Mr. Larson, who coached basketball and taught the shop class. I took shop and finally put together a scrubby looking magazine rack after fiddling around on it for four months. Half the time the other lads in that class distracted me and each other by talking sex, and so we didn't get much work accomplished.

In shop we were also taught how to turn out wooden figures on the lathe. One day while I was botching up a candlestick on the lathe, the pivot point where the metal met the wood emitted an ear-piercing squeak, and I yelled out, "Holy Jerusalem." So I got the nickname, "Jerusalem." I certainly picked up some inglorious nicknames in my youth. Later on, the process didn't stop. In the seminary I acquired the name "Vermin" as a takeoff from my real name, "Vernon," and you can't get much worse than that. Not so long ago at a meeting an outstate bishop called me by that choice appellation. It seems that one of his priests who was a classmate of mine in the seminary had apprised his prelate of my nickname. Well, at least I'm not ignored.

In the second year of shop class we learned something about overhauling a Model A Ford engine, but not much. Later on, when I attempted to overhaul the family John Deere tractor that fact became apparent. In a later chapter you will read that sad tale.

The school fielded no football team then, and as far as basketball was concerned, that was out because the Lord High Agriculturist at the Schaefer Chateau made it clear that if I wanted to eat I'd better make up my mind to lend a hand in agricultural production after school hours and forget about athletics. A wise decision in view of the fact that my athletic prowess was nil and more suited to plodding along with a pail of cracked corn for the chickens. The school sponsored a sporadic physical education course. All I remember about it is sparring around a few times with boxing gloves during which I picked up a bloody nose now and then. In order to preserve the integrity of my proboscis thereafter I decided to use my noodle a bit by promoting some diplomacy with my sparring partner and convince him to do more faking with the gloves and not take the sport too seriously.

Mr. A. J. Noll was superintendent, and a very nice man. We didn't see him around much except when he popped into the assembly room and whispered messages to students at their desks and strode out again. I often wondered what kind of messages he was transmitting. Finally, he stopped at my desk to transmit one, the only one in my whole high school career.

Pa had called up the school to inform us that we were to stop in at the hospital on the way home from school to pay a call on Ma, who had had another baby. Darlene Mae Elizabeth was born November 6, 1935. Her arrival was a bit of a surprise, since Ma never advertised the fact that she was to present us with a new sibling, and I don't recall we noticed an increase in her girth previous to the event.

Darlene's arrival was like an afterthought because it was eleven years since a squalling new infant had graced out portals.

That was in 1924, when Magdalen was born at home on the Hartneck Place. The only reason I remember it was that Ma made a lot of noise ushering her into the world, but we were still too young at the time to understand the anguish the daughters of Eve experience when they give birth and so were a bit puzzled at the cries issuing from the bedroom. Actually, Darlene was the only one of us six who was born in a hospital.

Mr. Noll was a medium-built man, a bit inclined to portliness perhaps, dressed impeccably, and his greying hair was carefully combed at all times. I never could quite figure out at the time how a person could keep his mane so neatly plastered down on his dome because I could never plaster down my curls like that. As a matter of fact, I didn't even try.

Mr. Noll rarely gave speeches in the assembly room telling us it was time some of us bandits started shaping up. Maybe it wasn't his job. Anyway Miss Johnson took it upon herself to deliver such lectures when it was necessary to do so and managed to run a tight ship even though she was a female and obviously couldn't sock anybody around. She didn't have to. She had that gift of moral suasion or whatever it was. Without raising her voice very much she could convince the student body to act like ladies and gentlemen most of the time while around the precincts. What happened off the school precincts was something else—or, more accurately, what happened on them outside of school hours. We will give you one example of the latter.

One night in the fall of the year we sophomores put on the traditional initiation party for the freshmen, as was the privilege of the sophomores, while the seniors presided. During the affair the august seniors had posted their class flag on the steeple of the school to manifest their superior standing among the student body. This flag was nothing but a torn blue shirt. This was a challenge to us in the sophomore class to remove the banner of the seniors who were going just a bit too far in asserting their importance among the academic community. We determined to pull down the blue banner and erect in its place a white one just to take the seniors down a peg. The school colors being blue and white, there wasn't much choice in selecting the color of our flag. Besides white shirts were easier to come by than blue ones.

After the initiation shindig was over and the kids had vamoosed homeward and the janitor had locked up the fortress, we emerged from the "can" where we were hiding. Clutching our white flag we beat it up into the belfry to tear down the blue and hoist the white. From the inside of the belfry one had to gingerly claw his way up to the flag pole atop it. The belfry roof was a bit steep, and if we had slipped negotiating our way up the shingles, there probably would have been a free day from school so the student body could attend a funeral or two. But we got the job done without mishap.

I don't know what I was doing up there contributing to this escapade, since I was just a quiet farm lad who minded his own business, not even giving the girls much of a tumble, and who kept the Commandments pretty well for fear of going to hell. Nor do I recall who the other two or three Robin Hoods involved in the escapade were.

At any rate, the seniors were terribly humiliated to discover the white flag flying from the steeple the next morning when they proudly gazed up to salute their blue banner. It was their turn to hit for the belfry to redress the wrong, but I guess they were collared by the janitor, who wanted to know since when classes were held in belfries. Nobody in the administration even noticed the rag waving in the wind from the steeple. How many people look up into the sky in the morning? Maybe a farmer does to detect any evidence of his downed hay getting wet or a holy monk raises his eyes to heaven in prayer at matins, but the ordinary citizen never gets his eyes above the level of a first story window all day.

When the janitor was informed by the seniors that the educational institution was advertising its ideals by flying a dirty white shirt from its steeple he reported it to Mr. Noll, who prudently chose to ignore the whole affair lest parents get wind of it and he might find himself in a frying pan. He just made certain that come the next initiation party there would be no flag flying cere-monies before, during, or after, and so the tradition was very short-lived.

However, after we had accomplished this unique feat that night, we had to go somewhere to celebrate. Ordinarily in those days kids didn't celebrate in a way which would tend to disturb the peace, like burning rubber on city streets or engaging in public hooliganism outside of All Hallows Eve. So all we did was to pile into my Pop's car and drive down three miles to Okabena to Ma's Place, a favorite hangout for kids, because they liked to hear her squall when they asked her to serve them beer, which she would never do. We drank our coke after the usual joyful encounter with the old girl for some beer and went home to say our night prayers.

A further word about this high school initiation bit, which has fallen into disuse these days. It was a rather unpleasant affair for freshmen, and that was what it was intended to be, of course. Getting blindfolded and being forced to eat "brains" (cold macaroni), being forced to wear crazy clothes, and getting plastered with flour and water, and in general, being made a fool for the enjoyment of the upper classmen—such was the price one paid to be integrated into high school life. There was a lot more non-sense to it than what we have indicated, of course, and the boys of our class received an additional "treatment" nobody else knew about. We were taken down into the locker room and were greased with wintergreen on parts of our anatomy not usually held up to public view. It was a time consuming procedure, and rather ineffective, since the stuff didn't really sting as much as our tormentors hoped it would.

I never distinguished myself in any endeavor in high school except probably nobody else's feet smelled as much as mine. I never changed socks often enough, and I suspect I had about as bad a case of B.O. as anybody in the student body.

I did get on the Honor Roll, though, midway through the freshman year. In a way, it was a mistake to achieve that dis-tinction because once on the Roll, I had to stay on it or I wouldn't get the car. The honorable progenitors wouldn't tolerate loafing on the job, and if ever I failed to make the Honor Roll, that was proof plus I was loafing having once demonstrated my capabilities. It was dern difficult for me to get on the Honor Roll since I wasn't at all loaded with talent. So, once inured to studying, I got into the habit of it, and by sheer mental gymnastics, ended up third in the graduating class in scholastic standings. Evelyn Haberman was valedictorian and George Freking, salutatorian. Poor me, huffing and puffing and pushing my meagre gray matter to the limit, slid into third. Still if anyone had been betting on me like they do the horses, I'd have paid off for "show" at least.

Let us preach a moral here. I managed to learn how to study in high school, and that carried me a long way in future scholastic endeavors. I could have loafed, but now I'm glad I didn't. The tragedy is that those who do loaf through high school are legion, but it surely doesn't pay off. Maybe Earl Nightingale is right when he says that most people use only ten per cent of their intellectual capacity.

But I tried to distinguish myself in other extra-curricular activities. I went out for the class play, drew a part with two lines. I went out for the school operetta even though I knew I couldn't sing. Miss Christenson, the director, was kind enough to leave me in the chorus to make up a balanced appearance of males and females. That's probably the reason she left me in the mixed chorus too. In the school band I never got beyond second chair clarinetist. Let's talk about that band for a minute.

Pa loosened up to buy me a tin horn, that is, a clarinet made of metal instead of wood, because the tin ones were cheaper. Mine set him back $25.00, and with it I squeaked in various musical organizations for fifteen years without adding anything much to the total production of acceptable tone. But it was fun playing in all those different bands—high school, college, seminary, and occasional flings in a town band after ordination.

Along about the time I got the tin horn, Edgar acquired a cornet, and we both strove to make music in the kitchen while the others were trying to do homework in the dining room on these long winter evenings. The squeaking and braying coming out of the kitchen particularly disturbed Toots, who found it hard to concentrate on her studies anyway, and she whined and wailed considerably during these practice sessions. However, Ma and Pa must have had some dreams about Edgar and me becoming virtuosos some day and would not sustain Toots' objections. Eventually, we mastered the playing of "Lightly Row" and "Rock of Ages," and decided to form an orchestra, so we could give some competition to Lawrence Welk, who was then playing on WNAX, Yankton, S. D.

We organized a neighborhood orchestra, which I appointed myself leader of. There was Edgar on the cornet, Albert Mitchell, trombone, Arnie Iverson, bass horn, and Leonard Liepold and myself on clarinet. Eventually, after a few weeks Margie was able to pick off a few notes on the piano and joined the group. Once in a while when Toots was in a good mood and wasn't trying to make fun of us, we let her play the triangle, the only percussion instrument we had. After one winter of sporadic practice, we made our first public appearance, playing a few easy waltzes in a rather sick and lazy fashion. And what was the occasion of our first and, I guess, our only public appearance? The local Ladies Aid meeting in the church basement. Vernon and his Vibrant Voodoos mercifully went out of existence the following Fall when Vernon went off to college.

I tried to make myself a big name, unsuccessfully, of course, in another department during high school days. That was in declamation. There were three divisions: oratory, dramatic, and humorous. I selected oratory, memorized a speech on how much war cost, mumbled it through at local elimination and—got eliminated. Tried it again the following year with the same result. And that second year I had only one competitor in oratory, Tom Maloney, who didn't even do a good job of memorizing his selection, horsed around delivering it, and still was picked by the judges. And I was destined to be the mouthpiece of the Lord some day!

CHAPTER XIV

Commencement 1937

High school graduates have been sashaying up to auditorium stages for many decades to receive a diploma and the congratulations of the clan afterward. What was it like in 1937 when the taxpayers gratefully unloaded our class from the premises for good one hot evening?

It wasn't much different as far as the ceremony was concerned. Some speaker undoubtedly told us to go out and conquer the world and all that jazz, and we forgot everything he said ten minutes after the affair was over. The newest trend in high school commencements in the seventies is for two or three students of the scholastic upper echelon to give short spiels and call it a day. This is a distinct improvement. Nobody likes long talks from a stranger. Most of them aren't any good. The topnotch talent in high school haranguing costs the taxpayers too much. In our youth-worshipping society today a seventeen-year-old standing at the podium puts people into near ecstasy.

We didn't wear caps and gowns. That was an unnecessary luxury in the Depression, and I don't recall it made one whit of difference as far as we kids were concerned. We had been trained not to make any demands of any kind but to be happy with the cards we were dealt.

Our graduating ceremony took place in a brand new auditorium, and we certainly wouldn't have had that were it not for the WPA, a federal agency created by that great alphabet maker, President Roosevelt, to create jobs in the Depression. The local taxpayers certainly wouldn't have put up this new addition to the old educational castle. They were quite hard up, so you couldn't blame them for any intransigence in approving bond issues.

In 1937 unemployment was still a national scandal. Not for us on the farms, though. For instance, on Commencement day we pitched hay like an Israelite slave in Egypt all day in the broiling sun, and quit only in time to eat our frugal meal and wash our ears preparatory to going down to snatch the diploma. We probably had hayseed in our hair, but that's what we were. We certainly weren't educated dudes. Nobody can be considered to have acquired an education when he leaves high school. He might have acquired some education by the time he has reached the age of fifty. Then as well as now, some who trot up to get a diploma handed to him by the president of the school board are just capping off four years of loafing. He gets the diploma because the school district has no intentions of financing further loafing on his part. But, of course, then and now, most of the class had not earned that fancy-looking piece of paper.

We didn't stay out all night after the ceremony. In 1937 nobody ever heard of kids doing such a thing. We were allowed to stay out until 1 A.M., however, and that was something new, maybe the beginning of our permissive society.

First, we went home to smile at the relatives on hand for the affair and consume some ice cream and cake. That bit of protocol finished, we climbed into the 1935 Ford, the Schaefer family chariot, picked up a couple of other members of the flaming youth and motored down to Lake Okoboji across the border in Iowa where an amusement park was located, the mecca of sweethearts on parade.

We didn't get back home until almost three in the morning. When we left "Gusty" Freking off at his farm, he was scared that his Pop might wake up, look at the clock, and come charging out on the porch with a mop handle in his hand.

The next morning, right on schedule, we had to go out and cultivate corn, I fell asleep, plowed out some corn, and went through a fence with the John Deere tractor. It wasn't the first time, but only the first time I did it before noon. On other days after noon dinner we always go sleepy on that rig and tore up a fence now and then.

Commencement was the end of a nine-month vacation. We always regarded high school work as a picnic compared to working in the fields.

One day in May of 1937 as I was walking home from school I was contemplating the possibility of finding an easier way to make a living than farming all my life. On an impulse I stopped in at the rectory to have a talk with Fr. H. A. Boecker for the purpose of finding out in a somewhat guarded fashion (I didn't want to stick my neck out and get signed up) what the seminary might have to offer to alleviate my aching back. But it happened anyway. The next thing I know, he had signed me up for the fall term at St. Mary's College in Winona, the place where all the lads who were contemplating the priesthood went for prepartory work. The priesthood turned out to be a real deal, and I would advocate it for any number of lads clattering off the stage with a diploma this spring. The Lord gives you so much for what little you give in this vocation.

In 1937, we were still in the Depression, and F. D. R. was President. Despite his other efforts he couldn't get us out of the slump, so he took us into World War II, and that did it. A few Presidents since have done the same thing for the same reason, but none are likely to get by with it anymore in the future.

In 1937 the auto industry was beginning to discover they could hoodwink the public by instituting annual model changes, namely, bending some sheet metal here and there instead of concentrating on sound enginering and safety features. We were taken in too, and found it very difficult to be happy with last year's model. Chevrolet was about to abandon the "knee action" suspension while Ford was introducing the optional 60 h.p. economy engine along with the standard 85 h.p. version. The little engine went over like milk in a German beer garden. The horsepower craze was beginning. Even with 85 h.p. the cars went much too fast for the roads, and the disgraceful era of highway slaughter was under way. America was not to see the emergence of sensible automobiles again until the beginning of the seventies and very little in the way of safety features until then. Of course, the foreign cars sold in the country for a decade before then gave the buyer an option to acquire something which made sense in the way of economy and handling.

We had Junior-Senior Banquets but not proms until our last

year in high school. Then we lads pondered how we would ever learn to dance for the occasion. Clarence Abernathy hit on the idea of converting this unused brooder house into a dance hall and inviting some girls to do the instructing. And so it came to pass. The chicken shack was the site of regular Friday night dances for teenagers the rest of the summer. The "Cafe de la Chicken Coupe" as we named it, overlooked the large smelly Liepold slough, but when the moon came over this huge frog pond it seemed very romantic. You know, kids don't really have to have nearly as much as you think they do in order to be happy.

Springtime on the Farm

CHAPTER XV

Hatching and Planting

This was the era of the Depression, between 1932 and 1937. The snows had melted, filling up the numerous sloughs. Nobody drained sloughs then. First, they didn't have money to tile them out, and secondly, everyone had enough land as it was in view of the limited equipment they had. Nature stayed in better balance too. We are beginning to rue the day when we decided to drain all our wetlands.

Jack Creek ran bank-full on is curvy way to Heron Lake, sometimes spilling over into our low-lying hay land. Nearby Duck Lake, a smelly swamp in midsummer, lapped right to the edge of the road running north out of town toward the land of the Norwegians around Storden and buried a forest of cattails which grew during the low water mark of the previous season.

It would be some time yet before Leonard Liepold, the neighbor kid, my brother, Edgar, and I could raise the boats of the duck hunters, cruise around all summer with them inspecting duck nests in the tall grass and put them back before the frost was on the pumpkins.

Often as we walked to town for Holy Week Services to serve as altar boys, water from the spring thaw ran in rivulets everywhere while the roads were laced with deep ruts as the frost came out. There were few hard surfaced roads in those days, but the Model T and Model A Fords with their high clearances negotiated them fairly well.

Not long after Holy Week was over, we'd have to be out in the granary every evening cranking the fanning mill which cleaned oats and barley for spring planting. The flat hoppers clattered as the sifted the seed about, filtering through the heavier mustard seed while the blower took out the quackgrass seed and whatever debris was lighter than the oats. It was an awfully dusty operation, and I wheezed and choked like our dog, Boots, after he'd done battle with a skunk. Pop had to have so many sacks ready for the next day's sowing, and so we had to crank them out as the robins sang their vespers. The horses, Tom, Queen, Prince, and Nancy were hitched to the grain drill, and the seed was planted right into the disked cornstalks. Amazing how it grew into waving fields of grain by July.

The grass was greening, and the cows were turned out into the pasture again which meant we had to tramp out to "get the cows" every morning and evening before milking. Boots was of some assistance when he wasn't distracted by a rabbit or sniffing into a gopher hole.

Tender young dandelion shoots were dug up by Ma to make salad for supper as greens from the garden were some time coming yet. In fact, it hadn't been plowed yet, and she was nagging Pa to get it done. Since it was hardly a half acre in size yet produced an abundance of food to carry us through the winter, Pa plowed it with an old hand plow and one horse like Grandfather used to break the prairie.

The first batch of eggs laid in the tray of the kerosene incubator were beginning to hatch, much to our fascination as we watched the process. We had easy access to the incubator since it was installed right in the dining room and smelled up the house a bit with kerosene exhaust fumes. That's how the lesson of Easter was taught us—the baby chicks pecking their way out of their shells symbolizing Christ emerging from His tomb. At least, that's what Ma said.

The hens were released from their winter captivity, and, among other things, were rustling around in the ash dump dusting their feathers on sunny days. The roosters were chasing the hens around the yard, and when we asked Ma what they did that for, she wouldn't tell us. Once liberated from their winter quarters in the damp tile laying house, the birds, as a gesture of protest perhaps for being incarcerated in that uncomfortable shack all winter, started laying eggs all over the farmstead instead of continuing to use their nest boxes within the building, and every day after school we'd have to go on an egghunt to find their secret nests in the barn, under the granary, and under the tool shelves in the garage. Some we didn't find, eventually an old "cluck" would emerge from her hideout with a brood of baby chicks later in the spring.

Since the production of baby chicks from the incubator was usually insufficient Ma would "set" a few hens in rows of boxes upstairs in the granary to hatch out eggs using Nature's method. We had to lug grain and water up there for their sustenance during this gestation period, and once in a while would steal our hand under the hen to feel of the eggs at which the annoyed bird would inflict a rather painful peck on our paw while angrily clucking in a deep-throated manner. Hence, they were called "clucks." After the clucks hatched their quota, they'd take off with their little chicks around them, somehow manage to get down the steps with them and start scratching around the yard and barn to provide food for the baby chicks. To watch an old hen scratching was fascinating to me. She'd pivot on one foot while tearing the surface with the claws of the other and reverse the process, then look around to see what she had unearthed and peck away, clucking at the baby chicks to get busy and pick up the hayseeds and so forth.

Boots, the dog, got spring fever and would start on his nocturnal forays with his female dog friends, and I guess sometimes they chased sheep too. More than once he came home with a load of buckshot in his rear end. After a few days of recuperating under the granary, he would be back in circulation again. Then we would place him in front of us and give him severe lectures on the evil of his ways. He would sit there listening very attentively, licking his jowls, and offering a paw as a gesture of repentance, but always went back to his life of sin.

Meanwhile, Pa was testing corn for germination by planting some in a peach crate and putting it behind the stove in the kitchen. This irked Ma and the girls (we had three sisters), but there wasn't anything they could do about it. You didn't buy seed corn much less hybrid which I understand was being developed about that time. You planted your own corn and were happy to get 35 or 40 bushels to the acre yield. Fertilizer? It all came from the barn. There wasn't much overhead in farm operations then.

The previous year's cornstalks were disked down and the grain was drilled in without further ado. Today they plow under cornstalks after shredding them a bit with another expensive machine. In a crop rotation system, the previous grainfields had been plowed in early fall and had to be "quack-dug" before corn was planted. It seems our chief agricultural nemesis was quackgrass, and its roots had to be dug up, scattered on the surface to dry out. Thistles were another headache which came with the fall of Adam and Eve. These were called "Canadian thistles" and if not eliminated grew thicker than hair on a dog's back choking out everything else. There were two other varieties, the "sow thistle" which grew here and there and reached five feet high, and the "Russian thistle" which afflicted the farmers in the Dakotas. Neither of the latter two varieties bothered us too much. We hoed thistles by hand through the summer and found out first-hand what the Bible meant by: "By the sweat of thy brow thou shalt eat thy bread." But what the Bible writer didn't know about was 2-4-D and other assorted chemicals they spray on fields these days to get rid of noxious weeds of all kinds. Of course, we never heard of those chemicals in the thirties.

The quackdigger, or field cultivator, as it is now called, was the newest machine we had on the farm, and it required more power to pull than anything else on the farm, including our two-bottom plow, which could be dragged by our four horses and was for many a day in August while this little urchin sat on it dreaming dreams all day. You had to set the quackdigger down rather deep to be sure to get out all the quackgrass roots. Since our horses were not up to this operation, one day Pa bought an old used Samson tractor. The first day he hooked it up to the quackdigger and "socked" it into the ground the old Samson blew a rod clear out of the engine block. Pa was disgusted, after addressing many a choice German phrase at it, he left it sit out there in the middle of the field for two years and we farmed around it.

Next, he tried an old Fordson which he picked up for around twenty-five dollars, but it ran too hot and steamed like a miniature locomotive after a few rounds in the field. Furthermore, it was an impossible bugger to get started, and Pa more than exhausted his German vocabulary cranking it. You see, Pa used to cuss in German so we wouldn't learn any bad words but otherwise talked English. The Fordson soon ended up behind the chicken coop where it stayed until somebody got up enough ambition to tow it to Miller's iron scrap pile in town. Meanwhile, Ma harangued considerably about money wasted on "worthless tractors" and vowed if Pa got another one she'd throw him out and he could go back to the Dakotas where he came from.

Without her knowledge, about a year later Pa bought a brand new John Deere Model B in 1936 but kept it hidden on the other farm, a quarter section we rented south of town some three miles away. He got it from Seleen's Implement for $789.00, and it included a bolted-on, two-row corn cultivator. This was the pride and joy of Edgar and myself for we were tractor crazy much like the young chaps today are sports car crazy. We had to heckle him for four years, though, before he equipped it with rubber tires. We never succeeded in wearing out this plucky little tractor, and still had it when Pop quit farming in 1950.

On Saturdays we'd be out in the chilly spring wind disking or quackdigging, stopping once in a while to hover around the tractor exhaust in an effort to get warm. Spring didn't always stay once it came. Since the John Deere wasn't quite up to the load of the quackdigger, we'd have to drag along in the lowest gear and managed somehow to get the job done while the little two cylinders barked sharply all day in the unique rhythm of that machine which was always music to my ears although the kids whose dads had Farmalls with four cylinders tended to make fun of it. The favorite pastime of farm youth in those days was arguing the merits of various makes of tractors.

Talking about the vagaries of spring weather, it was on May 3rd, 1936, when we went to the nearby town of Worthington, Minn., to participate in the music contest, and a severe spring snowstorm came up during the day to block us in Worthington for the night. I still don't know what I was doing in the high school's mixed chorus, since it was proven I was incapable of singing the scale when I was challenged to do so for chant class upon arrival in the major seminary. But I was great for bluffing and even got into the church choir because I preferred roosting in the choir loft during Mass when I wasn't serving. In the mixed chorus it was only a matter of letting classmate George Freking handle the tenor part. The simple fact was that it was more fun by a long shot to be bluffing along in the mixed chorus than to be sitting out on that tractor freezing to death quack-digging on Saturday.

Pigs farrowed in the spring, and no homework was done those nights as we hovered around the pens to help see that all was going well, and that the sow wasn't about to accidentally "lay" on a couple of her young. This was one of the largest sources of piggy infant mortality. If a little pig or two looked like it might not make it, we put it into a straw-lined bushel basket, brought it into the house, and put it behind the cookstove. Again Ma and the girls didn't like that at all but somehow, because they were females, they soon became attached to the little creatures and didn't seem to mind feeding the baby pigs with a bottle. Why we labored so hard to preserve a few pigs which were next to worthless on the market, I'll never know. I guess it was just the thrift ethic most farmers had, and the eternal hope they always possessed that maybe this year prices will be better. Even now, with farm prices lower than ever, they still haven't gotten over what has turned out to be an almost impossible dream.

Soon corn planting time arrived. The corn was "checked," that is, it was planted with a two-row horsedrawn rig which followed a wire stretched down the length of the field. Every time it hit a knot in the wire, it "checked," namely, dropped three kernels into the ground at a precise spot known as a "hill." If you did it right the corn could be plowed both directions, lengthwise and crosswise. It was the only way to control grass and weeds between the rows. No herbicides yet, you see. And if somebody had said that some day farmers would be dumping a slug of fertilizer with each seed we would have been very puzzled. Pa didn't let me plant corn because he didn't trust my abilty to do so properly, and wise he was in that assumption. My whole agricultural career as a youth involved mostly goofing things up or wrecking machinery. I was not slated to be a tiller of the soil as much as I have always loved rural life. He did let me drag the fields before corn planting, though. With four or five sections of drag behind the John Deere that didn't take very long and so met with my wholehearted approval. A drag with its rows of teeth combing the field tended to pulverize the soil somewhat for a better seed bed.

After the garden was planted and began to sprout the vegetables (which were sorely needed for sustenance throughout the year, as we couldn't afford to buy canned food) the chickens were attracted to this plot of ground for easy scratching in the soft, well-tilled soil. They also attacked the flower beds in the houseyard with great gusto. Sure, this area was fenced off, but they would fly to the top of the fence and jump down the other side. The Leghorns were especially adept at that, but the Rock Island Reds were a bit too heavy to get airborne that high. We always had a certain percentage of Leghorns because they were the best egg layers. Chasing the chickens out of the yard got to be too much of a prosaic chore, so I'd sit on the steps of the porch with a BB gun, and when a hen flew to the top of the fence, "plink" she'd get a pellet stinging her in the gizzard and would retrace her course.

And the next thing in the spring we would see Pa sitting in the cellar cutting up potatoes for planting. One "eye" or bud was all that was needed for each potato seed, but he usually left two on each piece in case one konked out in the ground. The following Saturday I'd be straddled on the rear end of the potato planter slipping one such piece of potato into each slot as it went by. I never lasted at that job very long because too many slots went by me before I could slip one in, and "Toots," my older sister, took over at the command of Pop who was driving the team of horses down the row but always glancing back to see how the offspring was doing—or not doing. I guess I was already then given too much to meditating on the Gospel all day to pay much attention to mundane agricultural pursuits. Only Pa called it "daydreaming." Actually, I was having visions. Well, to be honest about it, they weren't visions of the Lord appearing above the willows by the creek, but visions of barrelling down the road in one of those classy Packard roadsters with white-walled tires and a graceful eagle on the radiator.

Finally, in the spring, vacation ended when school was out in June. Then we had to go to work toiling all day in the fields instead of fooling around in the assembly room in school, although I did work hard at studies. Had to, because Pa wouldn't let me have the car if I got off the honor roll, and he never realized how difficult it was for this dumkopf to stay on the honor roll.

On the farm you learned to work hard for no pay, and when you returned to school again in the fall, you were as bronze as an Indian and tough as a prize fighter. How we got that way exactly will be detailed on the next section concerning summer on the farm.

CHAPTER XVI

Company Comes

In the summer months guests came on Sunday, and the host entertained them for dinner. Dinner was at noon, not in the evening like it was in fancy society. Our evening meal was always "supper."

Relatives were our chief guests for Sunday noon dinners. When they sent word ahead they were coming via a letter bearing a two cent stamp (a red one with a picture of George Washington on it) we had to go into action on Sunday morning. The only remote preparation consisted of Ma baking a batch of kuchen on Saturday afternoon.

Upon arrival home from Mass we went out to try catching a rooster or two to provide the main course. Since roosters are fairly agile, you didn't just go out and grab one by the wing or neck. You used a hook. This was a long thick wire with a small shepherd loop on the end of it. With it you could hook a rooster by the leg when he wasn't on guard. I used to enjoy hooking roosters, because they seemed so cocky and proud, the way they carried themselves about and sort of reigned over the hens. And sometimes they would chase me when I was a little laddie, and I didn't appreciate that.

Grasping the struggling fowl by the legs, we dragged the unfortunate creature to the chopping block out by the woodshed, where wood was chopped for the cookstove. With one hand you swung the condemned chanticleer up on the chopping block, with the other you grabbed the axe, raised it to a point above the rooster's neck, and let it drop. The weight of the axe was usually sufficient to sever the rooster's neck, and the headless creature would hop around on the ground with reflex motions, I suppose, and finally lie still.

The next thing on the program in preparing for the coming of company was to make ice cream. That would mean first a trip into town to get some ice. We piled into the Model T which now during the summer months had its top down, and Pa drove up to the ice house located behind the Bohnenpohl Meat Market and across the narrow alley from the city hall, which became the Majestic Theatre when the talkies arrived. This massive unpainted warehouse contained blocks of ice liberally sprinkled with sawdust. Fifteen cents worth was usually enough to make a batch of ice cream if you beat it home before too much of it melted. You wrapped the hunk of ice in an old blanket, put it on the floor in the back seat area and went hellbent for home.

One time Pa was doing just that—going hellbent for home in that Model T with three or four of us offspring scattered around on the cushions, and he didn't see the freight train bearing down on the village from the south. Usually these "Big Mikes" as we called those large freight locomotives, whistled so loud and long it was enough to wake up the dead, but Pa was preoccupied with some daydream or other and didn't hear the warning of this monster before she charged down on the crossing. When he did, he threw the Model T into reverse, (the normal way of stopping the early models of the T series; brakes weren't any good). We came to a stop a bit too close to the track. Something on the engine hooked the tip of the front fender which stuck straight out ahead and ripped off the fender completely, depositing it on the right of way further down the tracks. Pa hoofed it down the track after that freight typhoon had disappeared around the bend at the lake and had angrily spit on toward Windom, howling with awful agony every few minutes as it approached another crossing. He retrieved the fender, bolted it back on as soon as he got home, and told us to keep our mouths shut about the whole business lest Ma find out and raise Cain.

Well, how did you go about making ice cream after you got the ice home? Ma had prepared the ingredients and poured them into the metal cylinder, which contained a couple of quarts. The cylinder was dropped into place in the center of a wooden cask, and a gear mechanism slapped on top of it. Ice was chopped up and dumped into the cask around the cylinder, salt sprinkled freely about the crushed ice, and you started cranking to revolve the cylinder. While one of the kids sat on the cask to hold it down, the other cranked and cranked until he couldn't crank anymore because the mixture solidified. Presto! the ice cream was made. And the guys who cranked it into being were given the baffle from inside the cylinder to lick off. This homemade ice cream was very delicious, a real treat, far more tasty than the commercial product made today.

That about did it as far as preparing for company was concerned, on the part of us wee males, but Ma continued to slave over the cook stove while shouting orders to the girls to set the table and carry on sundry other little chores.

When Uncle Mitch, Butch, Elwin, or Aunt Nora arrived with their families, the menfolk were sometimes treated with a bit of illegal "moonshine" if we had some on the place. Uncle Thorval was a bootlegger, and sometimes left a cache of it in the granary when the law was hot on his trail. Ma forbade him to leave any of the stuff on the place, but Pa sort of liked the idea in order to have a snifter on occasion and helped Thorval sneak some in.

These pre-prandial drinks were not known as "cocktails" at that time. I never heard that term until after I got to college.

After the big meal (and we usually ate fairly well even in the midst of that fearful Depression, because we raised the food on the land and all the land exacted was perspiration, a commodity we had to exude whether we liked it or not) the company relaxed under the box elder or maple trees and talked away the Sunday afternoon. We kids hopped away to go down to the ball game where the Heron Lake "Lakers" were pitting their farm boys against those of Okabena or Storden in baseball.

Quite often during the summer months the clan would gather for a picnic. A picnic is dinner out in the open air, usually at some park by a lake. It meant packing lots of food and driving some distance, but not far really. It also meant that en route we'd have to stop at least once so Pa could take a bit of sandpaper and hold it to the revolving armature of the generator for a spell. He seemed to think that cured all the illnesses of an automobile.

CHAPTER XVII

We Break Beelzebub

The scene starts out being very, very sad. We are in our early teens, and obedient to parental command, we are slopping hogs. In part, feeding the hogs necessitated lugging a couple of pails full of this type of nutrient across a lot to an enclosure wherein a couple of expectant sows were incarcerated.

The feedlot we crossed abounded in pigs but also a few sheep . . . and one sheepbuck whom we will call "Beelzebub," and a mean critter he was too. Nothing pleased this abominable animal more than to come charging up behind an unsuspecting urchin loaded down with two pails of hog porridge . . . and WHAM! The hog soup flew in every direction as the poor farm lad in question was tossed forward into the mud, face first. His first sight upon returning to the land of the living was the startled eye of a grunting hog, which animal, however, wasted little time commiserating with the downfallen, but rather proceeded to slurp up what might have been left in the pails.

The poor victim (which by this time you may have guessed to be me) although destined for higher things in life, painfully struggled back to his feet and spat out a monologue which could hardly be classified as an after-dinner speech on the occasion of a nun's jubilee.

Wipe away your tears now, for things are about to improve. After both Sir Edgar and I had suffered this grave indignity several times in carrying out the duties of our state in life, we held a council of war and decided to teach Beelzebub that butting conscientious farm youth in the rear was a practice which would no longer be tolerated. However, since Beelzebub had a mighty thick skull (it felt like a fence post mallet in those unfortunate encounters), some drastic pedagogy was in order.

So it came to pass that one day we turned Beelzebub into a pasture on the south farm. A creek with steep sharp banks ran through this pasture. Edgar hid himself behind a tree by the creek bank, and I proceeded to walk nonchalantly toward the creek carrying two empty pails. True to form, Beelzebub came charging in to sweep the master's offspring off his feet again. Edgar peered around the tree, and, at the strategic moment, yelled the signal. I quickly side-stepped, and the son of a buck went charging on through—only to be confronted very suddenly with the creek bank and its abrupt drop-off. Attempting to brake his headlong charge only resulted in an awkward somersault off the bank. SPLASH! Into the drink went our avowed enemy while we both doubled over with laughter.

Beelzebub crept back up into the pasture, shook the water from his wool and resumed grazing. But had he learned his lesson? We had to find out.

Again the stage was set, and again Beelzebub took the bait only to be unceremoniously dumped into the creek again. "Persistent cuss, isn't he?" quoth brother E. Having enjoyed another protracted laugh, we set the trap for the third time.

The lesson had been learned. Beelzebub, panting after his second struggle up the steep bank, lay down to get some rest and to dry off in the warm sun, ignoring us completely thereafter.

This wolf in sheep's clothing, this tool of Satan, never again did crash his skull into the buttocks of the Lord's chosen ones.

With high drama such as this readily available, who says that growing up on a farm was dull business?

CHAPTER XVIII

Aunt Maggie Takes Off

In the late twenties, the women decided they should have the right to drive cars, but only a relatively few tried it. Aunt Maggie was one. Her name wasn't really "Maggie," and she wasn't my aunt. She was a distant relative whom we won't identify lest she comes out of her grave to whop me one over the head.

Husbands weren't very enthusiastic about teaching their wives to drive, so the poor gals never did learn how to drive properly, and the results were often quite sad.

Let's take the case of Aunt Maggie, quite nervous and about forty years old. She henpecked her husband until he went out into the barn and denounced her to the horses, but what she did to their new 1929 Model A Ford would have put Henry Ford into the looney bin.

The scene: Our yard on the farm. The time: Late afternoon. Maggie, who had been having coffee and gossiping with Ma most of the afternoon, decides it's time to go home, and she approaches the Model A. We little urchins gather around to enjoy the show.

She climbs aboard, and she's all business now. Scanning the dashboard until she finds the ignition, she turns it on and adjusts the gas lever on the steering column. The Model A had both the "footfeed," as we called it, and the manual lever. She adjusts this lever so that the engine, once started, will churn up some 3,000 rpm's. Then she fishes around with her foot until she finds the starter button on the floorboard and jams her foot down on that. The engine catches and sounds like a hurricane approaching, turning up such high rpm's. She looks up, smiles weakly as if to say, "Well, I'm kinda scared, but here we go!" Ma screams at us to stand back and give her plenty of room.

Maggie depresses the clutch and tries to shift into low gear. The gears grind and grind because one was whirring so rapidly with the engine, it hasn't had a chance to slow down enough to mesh with the other being applied to it. A mechanic would stop up his ears to be spared the agony of hearing a possible gear stripping operation.

Finally, she gets it into low gear. Her left foot depressing the clutch is jammed further down until it's half way through the floorboards as she grips the steering wheel very tightly and braces her body as if there was a 45,000-pound-thrust rocket engine in the rear ready to let go. But it's only a 55 h.p. four-cylinder engine about to throw its power around. Naturally, she released the clutch very suddenly. It doesn't kill the engine because the thing is turning over too fast. Having killed it so often before under lower rpm's, she had learned the necessity of always beginning with a high power setting.

The Model A leaps forward, it's back wheels digging in and spewing dirt and gravel back at some startled hens. Down the driveway she roars at 20 miles an hour in low gear, and the rig sounds like a hammer mill set to a fine grind.

Comes the T intersection at the county road, and its coming up fast. She slams on the brakes with her right foot, her left is on the clutch and both are pushed halfway through the floorboards or one would imagine they were from the way she stiffens straight out, applying pressure to her feet, and at 180 pounds Maggie can exert considerable pressure.

The car swerves to a stop in a cloud of dust. With the engine still howling at 3,000 rpm's, she repeats the original performance of getting the Model A into low, only this time she has to make a 90-degree turn after releasing the clutch. This churns up considerable gravel, but she makes the corner and is on the straight-a-way. She relaxes. After a while she decides maybe she should be in a higher gear. She depresses the clutch, and the gears grind worse than ever because, without realizing it, she is trying to get it into reverse instead of second. She finally decides it isn't worth all the effort and shifts in the other direction, and accidentally gets into high gear.

In high gear the Model A picks up considerable speed, and this alarms Maggie, so she pulls the gas lever clear shut. Once the momentum is spent, the car starts to buck as the engine is lugging at scarcely above idle. More likely than not it bucks the rest of the way home or to town in these low rpm's.

If she's going to town, here's how she parks on Main Street. She spies an empty diagonal slot, applies brakes full force, and practically stops on the proverbial dime with a little squeal of rubber on concrete. If anyone is following too closely, there would be some fracturing glass tinkling merrily, among other things.

She sets the power up to 3,000 rmp's again, and then comes the strangest phenomena of all. **She releases the clutch very gradually and slowly crawls into the slot!** That's when the thought first struck me that I would never be able to figure out women.

Aunt Maggie wasn't the only woman who drove like this. Ma did too but gave it up as a bad job soon enough. What a boon for women if those automobiles were equipped with automatic transmission in that era!

Summertime on the Farm

CHAPTER XIX

The Cat Ate Eggs

Out on the farm during the Depression, even though eggs brought only ten cents a dozen at the grocery store or produce station, it was nothing to be sniffed at. By careful management of the egg receipts Ma could about cover the household expenses which included most of the fabric we kids hung on our backs and the leather we put on our feet.

So when the supply of eggs was threatened by a cat on the place that developed an appetite for gourmet cat food found inside of eggshells, that purring creature was immediately marked for execution.

We kids took over the defense of suspected cats, but sooner or later Ma's eagle eye would detect a fat feline licking his jowls with relish in the chicken house after a meal while the empty plates, the eggshells, were still very much in evidence. She immediately passed sentence of death upon the creature and without mercy.

It wasn't that Ma was much given to destruction of life or cruelty to animals. On the contrary, she often berated Pa for losing his patience with cows and horses and whacking them a few good ones with anything handy once in a while. And she felt much distress when she heard a hog loudly protest as we laid hands on it in preparation for a bloody sacrifice under the box elder tree. However, when cats threatened to upset her household budget by eating eggs, she saw red. Her family came first. Cats were expendable.

With a determined look on her face, she'd march to the granary, procure a gunny sack, pick up the guilty cat, thrust it inside, and drown the creature in the stock tank. I don't think she relished the role of executioner, for when we reached the age of ten, she commissioned us to assume that role.

But neither Edgar or I had any stomch for drowning cats, even if they did dine on eggs.

Alas, one day our favorite tomcat was indicted and sentenced to death after his tastes became too expensive. The command came from on high that we proceed immediately with Tom's execution.

Edgar and I adjourned to the barn to hold a conference. We decided to make an appeal in behalf of the condemned cat. We proceeded to the kitchen and argued that since the cat was not familiar with the seventh commandment on stealing he shouldn't have to pay the supreme penalty, and that perhaps incarceration for a few months in the granary might rehabilitate the errant pussy.

To no avail. The judge was adamant. Eggs were too valuable. And furthermore, Tom received sufficient nourishment during milking time when we generously ladled it out for the whole tribe of kitties. The judge also ruled that the place was being overrun with mice, and if Tom weren't so lazy he'd catch a few. It became obvious that Her Honor would not even hear of any appeal for a stay of execution.

Another conference was held in the barn. The counsel for the defense agreed there would be no drowning. It just wasn't sporty to drown a cat. We determined to shoot Tom.

Edgar picked up the guilty cat out of the manger where he was snoozing, and we headed for the garage where Pa kept the family artillery, an ancient double barrel shotgun which packed an awful kick and was never used except to fire warning shots at chicken thieves or to pump lead at dogs caught chasing our sheep. I had never fired a gun before, and if Ma, who had an unholy fear of guns, knew what her offspring was up to, she would have come running and sounding her siren.

I lifted the shotgun off the bracket, inserted a shell into each barrel. Why two, I don't know. I remembered Pa had dispatched an ailing horse with just one. But as it turned out, this excess ammunition saved Tom's life.

Edgar was instructed to drop Tom on the ground and move away. The cat stood where it was dropped and curled and uncurled its tail in a very relaxed fashion while casually glancing up at the double barrel being zeroed in on him at a range of about two yards.

I cocked both barrels and quickly yanked the trigger.

Both barrels went off at once, knocking me flat on my back. The cat, what happened to the cat? I missed my target completely due to the frightful recoil. Edgar said Tom took off like a flash, cleared the board fence and disappeared.

Tom must have guessed that our last exercise with him was not intended for the improvement of his health, and we never saw him again.

After Ma recovered from her fainting spell, she appointed Pa as the new executioner of egg-eating cats.

CHAPTER XX

The Garden

Our garden was about a half acre in area exclusive of the potato patch, and from it came a considerable portion of the food which fed our family during the Great Depression.

Large vegetable gardens or even small ones you hardly see anymore in this affluent age. People say you can buy canned goods cheaper than you can raise it. They say that because they have money today. In the Depression we didn't. But we had a lot of juvenile muscle power around the place, and there was no shortage of fertile soil.

Garden operations started in early May when, after some nagging from Ma, Pa got around to plowing the area with an old hand plow and a team of horses, an implement like they used in breaking the prairie. He also disked and dragged it, and then it was turned over to the kitchen department of the Schaefer Shack. This consisted of the manager and chief cook (Ma) and her assortment of quarreling offspring.

The packets of seeds had already been ordered from colorful seed catalogues which had descended upon the household via the U.S. mail when snowbanks still hid the chickenhouse from view.

When the spring zephyrs had warmed up the soil, out came the balls of twine, wooden stakes, and hoes. Long rows were laid out with the twine to keep them straight for cultivating, and the chief Botanical Engineer in her flapping bonnet and long dress ran shallow trenches along the twine into which the seed was deposited and covered with a bit of soil. Little stakes supporting the empty seed packets identified the brand of vegetable planted in that row or portion thereof.

There was lettuce, carrots, onions, radishes, spinach, swiss chard, cucumbers, beets, peas, and sweet corn. Tomato and cabbage plants had previously been sowed in small boxes, set on windowsills with a southern exposure while Mother Nature was still spraying the land with snow showers. These were transplanted into the garden after Jack Frost had vamoosed for the season.

The strawberry plants came up each spring by themselves year after year until they petered out and had to be renewed. "Ground cherries" as we called them, seeded themselves and came up helter skelter all over the garden. These were fairly delectable, and when the little Indians of the tribe were sent out to weed the garden during the growing season, they consumed the ground cherries as soon as they ripened, much to the displeasure of the squaw who had them earmarked for canning.

Immediately after the garden was planted, the Chicken Guard, consisting of all the ragged offspring on the place, was posted. The leghorn roosters and the pullets roosted and dreamt all night about the next day when they would scratch in the soft soil of the garden and devour the seed and the readily accessible earthworms found therein. So up to the top of the garden fence they flew and down the other side into their Shangri-la. From the corner of her eye Mother Hubbard could immediately spot a splash of white in her garden from the kitchen window, and the order to "chase the chickens out of the garden" was dispatched from the open window to any of the offspring within earshot. If a couple of members of the Chicken Guard were engaged in pummeling each other and didn't hear the order, it was necessary for the Queen to gain their attention by means of a swishing razor strap.

After a long winter without greens and before the garden became productive, the little ragamuffins of the tribe were dispatched to dig dandelions for supper salad. But soon a heaping bowl of lettuce graced the table after the little lassies "ished" a lot when sorting leaves which occasionally sported juicy caterpillars.

Then as summer drew on, came the fresh onions, radishes, spinach, and strawberries. The latter suffered considerable attrition from the patch to the table. It seems that the pickers and food processors prematurely consumed so much of the juicy product that it became necessary for the boss to reserve strawberry harvesting to herself.

A garden so large required periodic going over with a horse drawing a garden cultivator to keep the weeds down between the rows, and after some nagging the baron appeared with the pony to take care of the chore. In addition, of course, there was a lot of hand-hoeing and weeding to be done in the hot sun by reluctant juveniles who found themselves doing penance for their sins at a tender age. When the priest on Sunday quoted Scripture "By the sweat of thy brow, thou shalt eat thy bread," the little urchins would add under their breath, "How about radishes, lettuce, tomatoes?"

God always rewards lavishly with fruits of the soil those who bend the elbow manning the hoe, and soon the canning season was on to process the abundant produce of God's half-acre for winter consumption. However, the males of the family had departed for the most part from the cabbage patch to be occupied with the hay and grain harvest.

In the garden on a quiet summer morn female figures were bent over the pea vines extracting pods to be shelled in the shade of the box elder trees during the heat of the day. The kitchen range was fired up for the canning process, and without air conditioning, the domestic hearth became quite a sauna. As a result, evening meals were eaten outside picnic style quite often.

Pea canning was followed by the rendering of peaches, which were purchased by the crate after the director of the domestic exchequer found "specials" on them in some store or market, and this fruit of warmer climes was hauled home in the back seat of the old Chevy.

Next came the early apples from the orchard, to be canned as apple sauce while the smaller crabapples were canned whole. Sweet corn soon followed. The rows of filled "fruit jars" began to line the shelves of the basement again. The industrious ruler of the kitchen even found time to brew some beer, which more often than not exploded after it was bottled and frightened the cat, accustomed to mooching around in the basement looking for mice.

Once in a great while, like the summer of 1934, a searing drought threatened our garden, and the water brigade, consisting of the whole family, went into action. This was an evening project. Everyone piled into the family chariot, which pulled a trailer on which were a couple of wooden barrels used during the butchering season to scald hogs. The rattling chariot wound its way to Jack Creek, with the dirty faces of the Schaefer brood peering out the windows. Here a bucket brigade of sorts was formed to hoist the dirty water from the shallow stream to the barrels. This continued each evening until the Lord finally heard the prayers of the tiring irrigation crew, prayers earnestly recited each night at bedtime, and opened the heavens again to send rain down upon the parched earth.

The tall hollyhocks growing along the fence of the garden were in full bloom for some time when the tomatoes became ready for canning. School started again, but still the tomato canning went on until over a hundred quarts of it lined the subterranean shelves. What was left of the ground cherries also found its way into Mason jars, along with the late apples and plums. Jam was made from currants and gooseberries we picked along the ditches while we were herding cows when the pastures dried up.

As Jack Frost began sliding in again from the north and the red October sky at sunset silhouetted flights of ducks descending to the swamp grass and cattails of Duck and Heron Lakes, the family crew was digging carrots to be stored in the basement bin. Also hauled in were cabbage heads which would be sliced on a cutting board and made into sauerkraut and packed into a big crock. Now the winter supply of vegetables was assured. The winter meat, however, still stood on the hoof crunching corn off the cob.

When the slough froze solid indicating meat would keep, one such porker would suddenly find itself facing a messy goiter operation under a box elder tree, and fresh pork chops were again piled on the platter for supper.

There is still one important foodstuff unaccounted for, the potatoes. They were there all right, forming the other half of

God's little acre. They grew and produced five hundredfold only because some ragged boys and girls regularly shook the orange squirming bugs off their vines into pails. In the process, mysteriously a few found their way down the necks of the little lassies clad in gingham dresses. The resulting shrieks brought out the baroness from her castle, and a couple of little male hirelings sought refuge in the hog house, hoping some lapse of time might quell the ire of said baroness. Potato bugging operations, although brought to a halt temporarily, resumed again the next day, and a couple of future priests found to their dismay that they had the whole operation to themselves.

In the fall, while duck hunters sprayed lead at unwary ducks in the nearby flats of Duck Lake, there were spinal aches in the potato patch as the fruit of the underground vines was docked from the ground and hauled into the basement.

Thus we bring to a close the Odyssey of the Garden. If Adam and Eve had taken better care of theirs, we would have been spared these many hours of toil in ours.

CHAPTER XXI

Cultivating Corn

Once upon a time, every farmer who raised corn cultivated it or "plowed" it three or four times. My scanning of farm magazines and personal observations while taking walks through the countryside indicates corn cultivating is getting to be a thing of the past. Now they squirt chemicals on to destroy the weeds and grass and probably destroy some wildlife too.

Before we were pressed into this business of cultivating corn, there was a short period in our early youth when we could sit on the banks of muddy Jack Creek and fish for bullheads on a June morning while the meadow larks serenaded, the blackbirds twittered but sounded terrible compared to the way the little wrens did it, and the bumblebees flitted from one wild rose blossom to another.

Alas, these few halycon days came to an abrupt end when Pa decided we could be more useful pulling wild morning glory weeds out of the corn. So up and down the rows we crawled on our hands and knees as we ripped up these tangling vines which put out nothing but a monotonous white blossom and tended to smother the young corn plants.

Whatever happened to the wild morning glory plants which used to grow in such profusion in cornfields? Another case of a better world through chemistry, I suppose.

I've always hated that plant ever since at a tender age we were pressed into what we thought then was abject slavery to pull them up day after day under the hot sun. We learned early in life that farming was no picnic for farm kids. The town kids —well, that was another matter. It seemed all they had to do all day was go swimming in the hole behind the brickyard at Heron Lake, and how we used to envy them!

Upon adding a few inches to my stature and a few pounds to my puny frame, I graduated into cultivating corn with a little garden plow pulled by one horse. Its little shovels dug up the soil between two corn rows. Edgar, being younger, rode the horse and steered it while I walked behind the plow and guided it. If the horse wandered too far to the right dragging the little plow too close to the corn row on that side, I'd holler "west," and if the horse got too far to the left, I'd holler "east," and it was Edgar's job to get the horse over in that direction so we wouldn't plow out any corn. But once in a while he would drift off to sleep on top of the animal, and my frenzied yelling would be in vain. There was no other recourse then but to pelt him with clumps of moist dirt.

He wasn't in a very good humor when he awoke to dirt stinging him on the ears or filtering down his neck, and he would slide off the horse to retaliate in kind. After considerable dirt flew back and forth while the puzzled horse stood patiently by waiting for hostilities to cease, we finally established a truce, and Edgar, thoroughly awake now, remounted the locomotive.

So it was that this dreadful procession continued up and down the corn rows day after day in early summer, and we'll never forget the feel of soft moist earth on bare feet.

Eventually, our legs grew long enough to begin operating a single-row cultivator drawn by a team of horses. With both hands and feet one would guide the bank of shovels on each side of the corn row while the reins were draped around one's shoulder. At least, one could ride on this contraption. Edgar acquired his own team and cultivator, and corn plowing didn't drag out quite so long anymore. Next came the two-row machine steered by pedals and pulled by three or four horses, depending on the make. This was the beginning of automation in farming.

The day of glory in corn cultivating came when we acquired a new John Deere Model B and its bolted-on two-row machine. However, the rhythmic bark of the two cylinders occasionally put me to sleep, especially after the noon meal, and once we awoke to the screeching of woven wire fencing. We undoubtedly powed out more corn with that machine than we ever did with horses.

The fourth time through the corn was the hilling up procedure, as you farmers remember. This could be done in higher gears. Across the line fence, the Kuhneau's had acquired a similar rig, and his kid and I got to racing each other up and down the rows of the tall corn. So, up came the plow by notches to reduce drag and thus gain more speed until the hilling discs barely touched the earth. Eventually, we resorted to pulling the governor on the engine to gain more rpm's. All this resulted in very little benefit for both corn and the engine, but it was great sport for a teenager who discovered there was some fun in farming once in a while.

Did the hard work on the farm, of which corn cultivating was only a part, hurt us any? Not a bit. The youngster growing up who has never known hard work in his formative years labors under a considerable handicap, I think.

CHAPTER XXII

Haying

"Whoa, whoa! . . . Bike, bike up!" The scene is a sweltering hot day in late June during the thirties. I had just deposited a sweepload of hay onto the fork of the haystacker and am trying to back away from the fork leaving the hay on it to be elevated up to the stacker and dumped on the growing haystack behind it. I don't know who started it, but when we wanted the two horses on the ends of the sweep to back up, like our predecessors, we'd bark, "bike, bike up" instead of "back, back up!"

No slave on the Southern plantations perspired more than the poor mortal whose job it was to run the haysweep on a broiling June day in Jackson County, Minnesota.

The day came when we graduated up to that job, and when the recording angel begins to note a deficit in my penance-for-sins column, I'm going to remind him to re-check those days in the hay meadows by Jack Creek. And I think there are plenty of you older farmers who can do the same thing—if not for driving a haysweep, at least for pulling apart hay in some oven of a hayloft.

The corn was being cultivated for the third time by yours truly, and fellow juvenile agricultural engineer, Edgar, on creaking rusting single-row plows behind tail-switching horses while Pop was sitting on a stone grinder, pedalling away to sharpen sickles. The timothy, quackgrass, wild roses, columbine and daisies comprising the wild hay stand in the virgin meadows by Jack Creek was maturing, and in a day or so the old Minnesota mower would be clattering away felling it for drying. The mower was made in the State Penitentiary at Stillwater, we were told, and there were days we'd have gladly exchanged places with the inmates who put the machine together.

The mowing wasn't so bad, and Pop did most of it while, if we got the corn plowed in time, we could get in a half day of fishing for bullheads in the creek before haying started. However, the bullheads were small. I don't know what happened to the nice fat ones we used to pull out of that creek in earlier years.

The raking wasn't so bad either. You were perched enough to catch the summer breezes, and it didn't take long with the eight foot swaths. The only unpleasant part came when one found himself raking over a wild bee nest. Then you'd have to take off like an antelope while madly batting away bees with your straw hat. However, occasionally a dive bomber would succeed in leaving a round or two of ammunition in your hide, and you'd writhe on the ground enthusiastically cussing in German like Pop always did, only you didn't know what the words meant.

Meanwhile, the horses, having gotten stung too, in the nose, the tender part of their anatomy, would take off in another direction, and we'd be lucky if they stopped at Freemire's or Jeppson's, the closest neighbors. Or, if we weren't so fortunate, we'd find them down in the soft willow grove with a wrecked hay rake. We never had a new hay rake. It didn't pay. Pop would usually pick up replacements for five bucks, and they were always so rusty, I never did find out whether they, too, were made up at the Pen or down at Moline, Illinois.

Finally came the hay stacking. Down the windrows you'd go behind the sweep, piling up the hay in front of you, hay which gave off waves of 110 degree heat upon your perspiring frame as you stumbled along hanging on to the reins. Once the load was built up, you could climb up and stand on the frame of the sweep to get some breeze as the rig rolled across the meadow to the stacker. This had its drawbacks, however. Occasionally the teeth of the sweep would jam into a good-sized anthill or gopher mound, and the rig would come to a very abrupt halt. This would pitch you headlong into the hay in front of you. No harm done except you'd get hayseed down your neck and get some more practice in German cussing. Sometimes it would snap a singletree or a tug on the horse's harness, and as you tried to repair the damage, the horse's tail would catch you full in the face a few times as it madly switched at the flies.

This did not bring out the best of your gentle disposition either.

After depositing the load on the big fork of the stacker and backing away, Edgar would snap the reins, and his horse proceeded to pull up the load on the inclined rails while ropes creaked under tension. Upon reaching the top, the load cascaded down in a burst of dust onto the stack where Pop stood half buried in soft hay. Not very often, but once in a while, we caught him daydreaming and dumped the load right on top of him. The Teutonic expletives would be considerably muffled, needless to say. I'm sure a member of the Third Reich would have found himself quite at home with the Schaefers during haying operations.

A pull on the crock water jug which was imbedded at the base of the stack, and we'd head out for another load. At three o'clock (Pop would always know the time by the position of the sun) we'd halt for lunch. Once in a while this would also include a bottle of Ma's home brew beer if it hadn't all blown up in the basement, and Edgar would have to dash off to the well where it lay cooling.

As the afternoon wore on the stack grew higher and began tapering. Lumbering across the meadow for the last windrows, we'd occasionally see a nest of pheasant eggs which hadn't hatched yet. The hen, sometimes fortified by the rooster, stood some distance away looking reproachfully at us. Or a mud turtle from the nearby creek sat withdrawn into its shell as we passed over. Once in a while we'd find a large snapping turtle and stop to tease it until it snapped off the end of the stick.

The stack finished, Pop would tie pieces of drain tile together with lengths of twine and throw them over the stack to anchor it. Maybe it was stack no. 4 with four or five more to go before we could get at hilling up the corn and repairing binder canvases preparatory to harvesting the flowing fields of oats and barley, now already headed out and waving in the breeze. It was a beautiful sight indeed, those waving fields of grain, but also a promise of more back-breaking labor when we'd have to shock it up.

CHAPTER XXIII

The Fourth of July

The Fourth of July—the day when, in 1776, a fledgling nation told an English king to go and peddle his tea elsewhere, and, according to a picture which used to fascinate me in the history book, a drummer, a fife player, and a flag waver marched down the street in triumph.

I remember how the 4th of July hardly had dawned when I was a young boy when the distant sound of a "blockbuster" going off downtown somewhere drifted in through the open bedroom window. It was a joyful sound because we had a few of them in readiness to explode too. They usually lifted a tin can quite a way into the air and elicited a sharp parental "Where did you get those firecrackers?" We were told that only naughty boys shot off firecrackers, and that they would have to write some day without any fingers.

On one Fourth one such blockbuster was set off underneath a wagon as it stood in the Farmers Elevator in Heron Lake. The startled horses took off, and sacks of hog supplement rolled out of the wagon's open endgate as the vehicle careened past the creamery, the fire hall, and on south toward Brewster. It was indeed a naughty boy who exploded that one. Still, nobody was supposed to be working on the Fourth—hauling feed, for instance.

Sometimes hay had been cut down and had to be stacked up, Fourth or no Fourth, but nevertheless I thought Pa was violating the sacredness of our freedom both as Americans and as farm lads by making us work on a national holiday. However, if work on the farm was not too pressing, we would rattle down to Okabena, a little village four miles away where the 4th of July was always celebrated, and I guess it still is to this day.

That was about as far as people drove to celebrate the Fourth in those days. There were a few in the village of Heron Lake who possessed a few extra coins of the realm and could afford a cottage on Lake Okoboji thirty or so miles away, and, of course, they went down there for the Fourth, and we all read about it the following Thursday in the "Local Happenings" section of the **Heron Lake News.** Having a shack on a pond somewhere was a status symbol even as early as 1933.

At Okabena there was the noon picnic in the park, the band concert, some sort of parade, and a politician was on hand to give out with the latest formula to end the Depression. He usually had a deuce of a time speaking because some naughty little boys were exploding firecrackers underneath the bandstand from which he orated. The people didn't mind because they figured his formula to end the Depression wasn't going to work any better than anybody's else's.

There was the inevitable tug-o-war between two teams of strapping farmers who grunted and groaned over the manila rope. And once they had a water fight too. It didn't amount to much because they had to depend on water pressure from the hydrant alone. Even if the Model T firetruck had been equipped with a pumper, the little engine would scarcely have had sufficient power to operate it.

Eventually, everybody got around to eating the noon leftovers for supper in the park and then went home to do the evening chores. These little municipalities couldn't afford to stage evening fireworks displays in the Depression.

These were pleasant Independence Day celebrations, and the community stayed pretty much together. Now people pile into their high-powered cars the Friday evening before the holiday and fight traffic to their cabins on the lake. Up there they drink beer, pollute the lake some more, and tear around in a high-powered speedboat, and then fight traffic all the way home, arriving there a nervous wreck.

We don't have many firecrackers explodng any more, but we have plenty of fiery crashes on the highways and mow down seven or eight hundred lives on the roads over the holiday weekend. Nobody cares much unless a wreck should involve somebody in the family or a friend. The fact that half of the casualties are caused by drivers fully or half looped to the gills with booze doesn't seem to excite anybody either.

Today the smart family stays home on the Fourth, has a picnic at a nearby park, relaxes in the afternoon, and in the evening leisurely ambles out to the south forty on the edge of town where the fireworks are held.

Those who are trapped in the big cities and who have no cabins in the spoiled woods to which to dash and get killed in the process, can spend the day looking at the classified ads for a farm in the country to buy before they go nuts.

CHAPTER XXIV

Summer Band Concerts

At one time there was a treasured summer institution in America—the weekly band concert in the park. Unfortunately, it seems to be disappearing in our fast-changing society.

Come with us to a summer band concert during the thirties in rural America.

The scene as we know it: a tree-shaded village park, one square block in area, situated in the middle of the village of Heron Lake, Minn.

In the center of this park was a screened bandstand. To one side of it was a row of swings, a couple of slides, and a merry-go-round for the kiddies.

Parked on the curbs around the parks on concert nights were the Model A Fords, the more low-slung Chevies, an occasional fat Buick, or an ungainly looking high-wheeled Dodge touring car, of 1924 vintage perhaps, which could jerk along at three miles an hour in high gear and pull a load of hay in high gear with higher rpm's.

It is Wednesday evening in late June Central Standard Time. Even without daylight saving time, the twilight usually lingered on until after nine o'clock.

The chores were done a little earlier on that day, and from seven to eight o'clock the gravel roads leading to town were churned into dusty thoroughfares as cars converged on the village. The whole family was packed into the auto, and sometimes in the case of larger families the car bulged with scrubbed up children peeking out from all sides.

For the trip to town dad usually kept on the same overalls he had been wearing all day, but he stuffed a clean shirt behind the bib. Sometimes he had shaven. More often he hadn't, much to the displeasure of his wife. Occasionally he left his battered straw hat at home, and on his brow was a sharp line dividing the protected white skin from the ruddy sun-browned lower part of his countenance and neck.

It was mid-week shopping night, and so first of all the eggs were unloaded at the Briardale, Robson, or Johnson stores to be traded for groceries. Mother was left on the main street to do the trading and gossip in a cluster of other women, to the distant strains of the National Emblem March or the Poet and Peasant Overture drifting in from the park.

Meanwhile, dad would try to find a parking place somewhere around the park to establish family headquarters for the rest of the evening. The children would immediately scatter but would be back once or twice to try wangling a nickel for an ice cream cone from one of the elders who might be relaxing and listening to the music in the darkening interior of the auto.

In the course of the evening, dad might stride down to Seleen's Implement for a while to get a part or put in an order for binder twine. Later he would be found standing around somewhere discussing crops with fellow farmers, and, of course, bewailing the farm prices which in the thirties were very low, but so were his expenses.

The little kiddies were busy squealing with delight at the slides or merry-go-round while the older kids were trying to show off on the swings by trying to arc higher than the top bar.

Nobody was really listening to the music except the older folk sitting serenely in their cars or mothers cradling their sleeping babies.

And the band played on. The opening march commenced around 8:15 P.M., and the final number, "The Star Spangled Banner" was played around 9:30 P.M. After each number, the applause took the form of horn tooting. This was a mixed caca-phony of sound comprising the beeps of the Chevys, the little electric klaxons of the Model A's, the weak calf cry of the few Model T's. The real performers were the big klaxons of the old Dodges. These were mounted on the side below the windshield and had to be activated by hand. They emitted a very sprightly, "AHH-OOO-GAH!" And we'll never forget the sickly soft sheep "baa" of the Oakland. Occasionally, some young buck with his hammed up Model A roadster had installed a trumpet horn, but he was usually cruising around town all evening with his girl and waking up the roosters.

With the last strains of the National Anthem dying in the air, there was a final burst of horn tooting, the groaning of self-starters, and the grinding of gears. But not all. In some cases, the kids had to be reassembled by the clarion calls of mothers, and sometimes, that having been done, there was no daddy. He most likely was still down at the liquor store engaged in animated discussion on hog vaccination or something over a glass of beer. Occasionally a burst of boisterous laughter emitted from the Pabst parlor indicating somebody had reached the punch line of a naughty story. Mommy would have to send little Claypoole down to this scene of activity to remind daddy the concert was over and it was time to go home.

And what were some of us teen-agers doing during the band concerts? We were inside the bandstand feeling like big shots and trying to make music.

I played in the town band most of my high school years tootling a tin clarinet. The better quality clarinets were made of wood, but then I wasn't a quality player, either.

I don't recall that anybody really invited me to play in the town band to begin with. I invited myself into the august combo because I heard that the members were given a free treat both after the Monday practice sessions and also after the concert itself. Possessing mighty few nickels for treats during the Depression, I decided to get in on a good thing.

So one Monday night I crept up to the second floor of the Fire Hall where practices were held. I was late, as usual. I quietly slipped into the last row of the clarinet section, and, by the way, that's where I stayed—through my entire career with the Heron Lake Municipal Band. The band was rehearsing "When I Grow Too Old To Dream," a song I'll never forget because of the circumstances.

It wasn't long before I sneaked little brother Edgar into the outfit too, as his tongue was hanging out in anticipation of those free ice cream bars. He had a cornet with which he produced severe distress symptoms in those listening to his renditions, especially the dog.

It proved to be of considerable benefit to my health to join the band, because previously during band concerts I got too many bloody noses fighting behind the produce station. Bernard Volk had a mean left, and my friend, Tom Maloney, tried but could never teach me how to parry it.

Handsome Lester Robson was the director, and Clarence Meixner, clarinetist, was the concert master who directed in Lester's absence. Both were very patient. Often we wouldn't get playing the march until the trio, but they never growled. You see, my fellow clarinetist, Marianne Peterson, was very fond of quoting poetry to me, and sometimes the poem lasted halfway through the number.

An eskimo pie was doled out to us after the practices and concerts down at Herb Mattison's Cafe. As we sat in a booth relishing every lick, Marianne quoted some more poetry.

Later on, during the concert intermission, special talent performed. This usually consisted of local girls singing love songs or warbling pop hits like "Lullaby of Broadway" or "When My Dreamboat Comes Home." Two of my classmates, Lucille Hartburg and Evelyn Haberman performed regularly. Very romantic.

One concert night the rear of the drugstore caught fire, and the chemicals stored there ignited and made like the Fourth of July. The band and everybody else rushed to the scene to enjoy the highlight of the whole summer season.

The village had acquired a new 1933 V-8 Ford firetruck the previous spring, and one day before school was out, they demonstrated its power before awed taxpayers by shooting a stream of water clear over the top of the old school. It was the first pumper truck we had, and the firemen could hardly wait for the first good fire.

Up to the scene roared the new red dragon sans muffler to give her more power, I guess. The zealous firemen rushed to hook up the hoses, the throttle of the V-8 was opened, but no water came out of the nozzle. They had hooked up the hoses on the wrong sides of the truck, and the pumper was shoving the water back into the hydrants! Almost blew off the top of the water tower.

Finally they got the hoses switched around. In the process they used language which made the old ladies swoon. With things hooked up right they disintegrated half the store with a powerful stream of water. We were terribly disappointed because they got the fire out rather quickly.

We never did finish the band concert, nor get our ice cream bars, nor poetry—nothing.

Brother Edgar always found himself sandwiched in between a couple of bigger girls in the back row of the cornet section. One of the girls was Dorothy Noll, the school superintendent's daughter, who was inclined to mother him a bit and show him where he was supposed to look in the book to play the right music.

So passed the glorious concert season held on the soft summer nights in rural mid-America.

Long after the concert was over the dust raised by the cars speeding homeward formed a silent beige pall over Liepold's slough. There the cattails, heavy with dew, bobbed slightly as if keeping time to the croaking of the frogs below while on the shore the crickets contributed their staccato cadences, and a loon mournfully complained to a marauding muskrat.

Ah, maybe we did get something out of all that poetry after all.

CHAPTER XXV

Trying to Overhaul the Tractor

"Now what do you think you are trying to do?" Dad was walking from the house to the barn, holding a freshly washed milker under one arm, and pointing in the direction of the tractor Edgar and I were working on with the other.

"Well . . . ah . . . Pa, we're gonna overhaul it. You said yourself last week it needed an overhaul job." I pulled on the wench, trying to loosen the rocker arm assembly bolt on the engine.

"Ach, dummkopfs!" he exclaimed. "Whatever gave you kids the idea you know how to overhaul a tractor? Listen, you two, if you can't get that thing back together so she runs again, by golly, you're going to cultivate all the corn next week with horses."

Edgar, 15, and I, 18, hated to harness horses and hated even more to drive them in front of an implement. We just had to do this job right! It was a simple two cylinder tractor, a 1936 John Deere Model B. We had watched mechanics work on this type of tractor downtown, and we had confidence we could do the job successfully.

Grumbling, dad walked on to the barn, deposited the milking machine there, got into his car and went to an auction sale. We didn't see him for the rest of the day. And for that we were very grateful, especially in view of what was to transpire later.

The job went smoothly enough at first. It took very little time and skill to disassemble the engine. We took the valves and cylinder head to Chatfield to have them ground and seated properly since we did not have the tools to do it ourselves . . . nor the ability.

By two o'clock in the afternoon the reassembly of the engine was about done. Valves had been ground, new piston rings installed, timing checked. But there was one item which caused us a bit of doubt. Should we have removed two shims from the connecting rod bearings to take up the slack caused by wear, or just one? We had removed two.

At three o'clock everything was ready to attempt starting the engine, but we found it wouldn't turn over. It was so stiff we had to use a crowbar locked into the flywheel to make even one revolution.

"Engines are always stiff after an ovehaul," I muttered confidently. "Once they start running, they loosen up fast."

But how to get it started?

Edgar came up with a brilliant idea. "Why not borrow the neighbor's tractor, haul our stiff machine up to the top of the steep hill back of the barn, let it start coasting down the hill until it builds up speed, throw in the clutch to get the engine turning, and she'll be barking in no time." Great idea!

Up the hill we pulled the newly overhauled machine, then turned it around and headed it downhill. I climbed aboard, and we were off! Halfway down the hill, I quickly engaged the clutch. The rear wheels had long spade lugs, and they dug into the sod. The tractor literally almost "stopped on a dime." From my perch behind the wheel, I catapulted forward and went headlong into a pile of hay which had been raked the day before. This broke my fall, and I sustained only a few facial scratches.

Two sobered and somewhat wiser lads went back to work and replaced one of the two shims we had removed from the bearings. Strangely enough, we got it started, and it ran very well until Pa quit farming, and the machine was sold at auction.

But, Lordy, we were so thankful that Pa wasn't around to observe that hillside experiment!

CHAPTER XXVI

The Holy Spirit and the Tractor

Would you like to know what, in the last analysis, triggered me into going to the seminary?

No, it wasn't a moment of gleaming truth while saying my night prayers, nor was it the words of a sage old pastor. It was, of all things, a blasted farm tractor. I wonder sometimes what would have happened to my life if tractors had never been invented.

It was a late summer afternoon, and I was sitting on this infernal machine plowing a field. This was on our hilly villa near Chatfield (the "Villa Campa Rivula" as I called it to make it sound like a snazzy place—using my expertise in Latin).

On top of a hill there was a badly eroded field, and we decided to plow it up and sow it down permanently. Even strip cropping or terracing wouldn't save it any more.

I was making the last round at the edge of this field where it began to slope sharply downward. One of the tractor's rear wheels was in the furrow, of course, and the other one on higher ground. On this slope it made the tractor lean at such an angle as to make a billygoat feel uncomfortable.

The rear tractor tire on higher ground struck a sizable anthill, and this jolt caused it to bounce upward. The trouble was that the wheel in question didn't come back down. The awful truth that an upset was in the making finally dawned on me, and instead of taking intelligent measures to save the situation, I simply took measures to save my hide. I deserted the ship with the alacrity of a jackrabbit.

Did the tractor tip over? You bet it did. In fact, it rolled all the way down to the bottom of the hill. Phlegmatic character that I am, I stood there and watched the whole performance as unperturbed as an owl in a tree watching a timber wolf devouring a ewe.

However, our troubles weren't over. Halfway down the hill the tractor ignited from the spilling fuel, and the turn-turtling tractor became a flaming pyre. That sight rather distressed me, and I plunged headlong down the hill after the rolling machine. By heaving considerable quantities of dirt upon the burning machine, I managed to put out the fire and ruined my carefully manicured nails in the process—"manicured," that is, with a jack-knife while listening to Kay Kyser and orchestra over the radio.

Leaving the scorched John Deere still belching thick black smoke and lying on her side, I sadly trudged home across the valley while trying to convince myself that every cloud must have a silver lining somewhere.

Pa was in the yard. "Did you finish the plowing?" he asked.

"Yep."

"Well, where is the tractor and plow?"

I pointed across the valley to the smoking ruins. "She tipped over, rolled down the hill, and caught fire," I glumly reported.

A look of deep disgust crossed his face. He threw up his hands, dropped them, and quietly sighed, "Ach, you'd better go to the seminary. You'll never make a farmer."

I had been thinking of going to the seminary. In fact, I'd been in to Bishop Kelly's office for an interview and passed his famous Greek test he was wont to throw at seminary candidates, and I passed it without answering a single question.

However, during the summer I had been harboring some serious doubts about this seminary business. Farming began to look pretty good to me, and blondes even better.

But somehow this day's events settled the question once and for all.

I never cease marvelling at the unusual operations of the Holy Spirit.

CHAPTER XXVII

Harvesting with the Old Binder

In the era of the thirties before emphasis on raising corn and soybeans, the main agricultural crop in the Upper Midwest was small grain as it was from the time the sod was broken. As a kid growing up on the farm in the early thirties, I never even heard about soybeans.

To harvest this small grain (oats, barley, flax, winter wheat) we used a machine we called a "binder." The rig cut down the grain and tied it into bundles. The McCormick Deering, made by the International Harvester Co., seemed to be the most common machine used. The Minnesota binder, made at the State Penitentiary, was also sold by most dealers in our area. We had a rickety old McCormick which cut a seven-foot swath and was drawn by four horses.

The innards of the machine, which made a lot of noise, were driven by a "bull wheel," as it was called. This wide wheel, equipped with lugs, propelled a master shaft by means of a large chain. From the master shaft, smaller chains propelled the other gear wheels which turned the canvas, the packers, and the kicker which threw out the bundle after the knotter finished tying it. This knotter, I thought, was an amazing invention. When it worked, it could tie a twine knot and cut it off from the rest of the twine in a split second. It would have taken me ten minutes to do it by hand.

The standing golden grain was cut by a rapidly moving sickle and lapped onto the moving canvas by revolving slats above. The grain stalks thus thrown flat on the moving canvas were picked up and elevated by other revolving canvases into the area where the packers would press it together while a strand of twine was strung around it. It was knotted and cut before the kicker came around and threw it on the carriage. After three or four bundles accumulated on the carriage, the operator would dump them on the ground by activating a foot control lever, leaving rows of bundles for us grain shockers to set up on their "buts" in order to dry out in preparation for threshing or stacking.

The twine was purchased in balls weighing three or four pounds each. Most of what we used was manufactured in the State Pen. It came in bags of four balls bound in burlap sacks and available at the implement dealer.

Before harvesting, the sickle was taken down from the granary rafters and inspected for worn sections. New ones were riveted into place when needed. That was Pop's job. I never flattened a rivet in my life.

Next, the canvases were taken down from their supporting brackets in the garage, unrolled, and checked for tears in the fabric, and broken slats were replaced with new ones. Without these slats the canvases couldn't move the grain along through the binder.

Once the two elevator canvases were installed, they remained on the machine throughout the cutting season. The leather straps tightening them around the rollers were loosened at the end of the day, and grain bundles were piled over them to ward off rain if a shower came up during the night or afternoon. The canvas which lay flat on the platform was always removed each evening. It could get soaking wet, shrink, and pull out the rivets anchoring the straps.

The day began early with cow milking, after which I'd have to go out into the pasture and round up the horses. Once in their stalls in the barn, they'd stomp their feet and wiggle the skin around their shoulders to get rid of the flies while you threw the harness over them and fastened it. This was a job I hated. In the summer months canvas covers were added to the harness to protect the horse's back from flies and other assorted insects which tended to make life miserable for a horse. These protective canvases became soaked with horse perspiration time and again and smelled awful.

Hitched to the binder, the horses dragged it around and around the field whacking down the beautiful standing grain which waved in the breeze. However, on a hot day, the horses would have to be rested periodically lest they overheat. It wasn't unknown for horses to collapse on hot days, but we never had that problem. Our horses were so lazy they wouldn't exert themselves that much. I think we had the slowest "plugs" in the state.

While the horses were resting, the binder operator refilled the twine box and oiled the moving parts of the binder with an oil can equipped with a narrow spout. Oil was squirted not only into the bearings but all over the housing, and dust accumulated on this spilled oil making for a mess of sludge over much of the machine. At least these parts of the machine didn't rust like the rest of it did since it was never housed in a machine shed. The day came when Zerk grease fittings were invented, along with the grease gun, to simplify the lubricating process. The only machine on our farm needing a grease gun was our new tractor acquired in 1936.

We now present a scene as we begin harvesting in 1936.

There was hardly a breeze of any kind. The sun, firmly anchored in the upper sky by now, poured down waves of oppressive heat. The stalks of golden winter wheat stood perfectly still, and there was a beautiful even stand of it in that eighteen-acre field. We should have had five acres cut already on this particular morning, but much time had been consumed replacing a sprocket gear on the binder.

The old McCormick binder had been rusting in the sun as it stood by the fence. By now in early July it was half buried in weeds growing around it and through it. This year for the first time it was to be drawn by a tractor instead of horses, so the new John Deere was backed into the weeds and hooked up to a new clevis where previously a tongue had been anchored to the top of the two supporting trucks in front of the machine.

Having pulled the binder out of the weeds into the open, we went to work on it. Perspiring freely, we tugged, grunted, and growled, getting the elevator canvases installed and finally the platform canvas. With sharp clicks produced by pressing on the bottom of the oil can, I doused all the bearings with oil without cleaning out the oil holes first with a piece of wire, so Pa would have to repeat the whole lubrication job after labeling me a "dummkopf." Two balls of twine went into the can aboard the "Harvester Express" and it was carefully threaded through the knotter. The sickle was installed, the tractor fired up, and off to the field of waving golden grain we went.

Nearby the larger oat field was beginning to turn amber. There would be no surcease once we got under way until all the small grain was cut and shocked.

It was a heavy stand of winter wheat, and the rickety old binder wasn't up to the strain of being dragged so relentlessly through heavy grain by that barking green dragon up front. Clink! and out went the sprocket gear on the first round. The boss on the binder expressed a few phrases of displeasure in German and instructed his engineer on the tractor to slow down and take it easy or the whole binder might collapse.

By the time Fred Seleen had found a replacement gear in one of his boxes out back, it was time to do evening chores.

The next morning by ten o'clock we were rolling again—not very far because this time the knotter wouldn't knot. By eleven o'clock we were able to get the temperature of the tractor high enough to switch from gasoline to distillate fuel. But all the time we were awaiting that angry call, "WHOA!" to come up from behind indicating that the binder had broken down again.

Still, all the grain was cut and shocked up pretty much on schedule.

In the evening, I took up the latest issue of **Country Gentleman** and studied with envy an ad of the new ten-foot power binder, called such because of a direct power take-off from the tractor to torque the running parts of the binder instead of the "bull wheel" doing it.

The power binder was never to see its full fruition in American grain fields because it was swiftly replaced by the combine, and how quickly thereafter farming became more and more automated! When I visit Machinery Hill at the State Fair these years I can't identify some of the farm machines anymore.

CHAPTER XXVIII

Shocking Grain

The horses stomped in their stalls and munched oats while their tails busily switched at flies. We grabbed the heavy harness off the hooks, one arm under the hames, the other under the rump portion of the maze of leather straps and fly netting. With a mighty heave we tried to get the paraphernalia on the horse's back, and in the process, we found we had tangled things up pretty badly.

It's a most discouraging sight then to see the tangled mess slide off the horse and drop on the ground. Pop, who in the meantime had swiftly harnessed Tom, Queen, and Prince, came around and gazed at the mess in the manure and, for the umpteenth time, ventured an opinion that I'd make one helluva farmer.

I, in my turn, ventured an opinion that we ought to get a tractor.

"What? With oats at ten cents a bushel?" he retorted with disgust.

Ten cents a bushel or not, there was a beautiful field of oats out there turning from green to amber and threatening to yield sixty bushels to the acre, a good yield for those days. The project at hand was to get those horses hitched up to the old rusty binder and cut it.

As usual, God had done His part and provided a bumper crop, and, as usual, the farmers were going to hazard a heat stroke to harvest it and then give it away to Archer Daniels or somebody. I didn't yet understand the hopeless marketing setup, but I did understand we'd have to go out into that broiling July sun and shock oats all day. That was a fact of life, and we didn't argue with facts of life.

When that old clattering McCormick binder got into that thick field of oats it would kick out bundles one right after the other, but all too often without tying them. It usually took about a half a day for that knotter to get into the swing of things. In the meantime, I, who was supposed to shock up the stuff, was also supposed to tie them by hand by grabbing a half dozen stalks, winding them around the bundle and fastening it. That was too much work. Besides, I was about as deft with my fingers as a two-year-old in a high chair. Of course, I made an attempt at it when Pop was looking. When he wasn't, I'd kick the loose stuff into a pile and set up tied bundles around it.

Edgar and I were supposed to keep up with the binder in shocking up the grain. We managed to do it when the binder broke down as it did often enough, or it was so hot the horses had to be rested every round or so.

As we threw the pungent smelling bundles into shocks, the perspiration poured off the brow, soaked up the straw hat and shirt, and gave us enough B. O. to nullify a ton of Right Guard. Fortunately, society hadn't become so soft yet that such things were worried about.

When shocking up barley, the barley beards tended to adhere to the perspiration and work down inside one's shirt. In protest at the added discomfort, we asked Pop why he wanted to raise the dang stuff anyway. He said Prohibition had been repealed, and it was needed to make beer . . . and shut up and stop complaining.

A few farmers placed a bundle on top of a completed shock, and I noticed a picture on the oatmeal box where every shock had a bundle on top too, but we dispensed with it. Pop said you'd have to place it just right or the wind would blow it off, and it would take us a hundred years to learn how to do it right.

As I toiled away in the July heat among the stubble, I looked up once in a while at the cars driving by on the Okabena road. The people inside the cars seemed so cool and happy, smelling like roses. I envied them very much, and decided that some people were just lucky, and some weren't, and no use making a fuss about it. In those days if a farm teen-ager was inclined to make a fuss, he might get a fence post wrapped around his noggin.

Even today, though, I miss that pungent smell of a binder

and binder canvases. A sort of combination of clean sweet oat smell, spilled oil around the bearings, and rust. Not oxidized rust from iron, but oat rust. We never cared much about the smell of sweaty horses, though. It was hot enough for the poor creatures without that canvas covering on their backs to protect them from the flies. In addition, their noses were encased in those wire meshed baskets to protect them from the horse flies which, when they stung a horse on its snout, would cause the distressed animal to toss its head around like he went batty of a sudden. We'd pat them on the forehead and console them in their misery, and they'd give us a sorrowful stare.

The crock water jug was set inside a shock to protect it from the heat of the sun, but sometimes we forgot to mark the shock and couldn't find it again. Then we'd have to forego a drink until we had shocked up to the other end of the field where we could step over to Jeppson's Stock Farm nearby and drink from the water pipe in the hog barn. The hogs snoozing on the cool concrete floors, didn't even grunt the time of day to us but kept wiggling their ears to get the flies off.

When the field was cut and neatly shocked up, it was a pretty sight which one misses today. Farmers looked at their neighbors' fields to see how thick their shocks were, and attempted to estimate the yield in bushels to the acre from the number of shocks.

Every Sunday the pastor would kneel down before the sermon and recite the Litany of Saints for a good harvest, and there was good participation. Farmers wanted a good harvest. But even after the bumper crop was shocked up, we still prayed for a good harvest when we should have been praying for good prices. Of course, the Lord helps those who help themselves, and there wasn't much He could do about it if the farmers were content to come into the elevator with a load of oats and humbly take what the grain sharks gave him.

I went away to the seminary and then came the combines and automation. The farmers started to go broke buying machinery and then had to have more and more land to pay for it. The farms got bigger, the farmers got fewer. The small towns dried

up. The cities grew and grew and began to stink. Youth became
soft and dissatisfied, took to drugs and fornicated. The country
was in a mess.

I'm glad I grew up on a farm when it was a way of life
which produced tough, tanned, stalwart men. Now agriculture
has become huge land factories controlled by land barons.

CHAPTER XXIX

Threshing Scenes

Farming isn't as much fun as it used to be. One of the reasons is the disappearance of the old fashioned threshing rig. We mean the big ones like Adolph Nimmerfro or Orville Peterson had. Adolph's separator was a 42″ Hummingbird of wood, and had two wing feeders. The Hummingbird was powered by a huge lumbering Hart Parr of two cylinders plus a heavy cast iron flywheel about ten feet in diameter. The entire length of the tractor was covered by a curving tin corrugated roof. In front was a large tin reservoir of water and a wide exhaust port. The Hart Parr would explode a couple of times in a rather uncertain fashion and then coast a bit on the momentum of the flywheel before pounding out a couple of more snorts. When under heavy load it exploded constantly and allowed itself very little interval for the flywheel to carry the load. It moved about three miles an hour in transit from farm to farm.

Orville Peterson, on the other hand, had a galvanized steel separator of 36″ cylinder, and on the blower was emblazoned in red paint the letters: "Red River Special." For power he used an Aultmann Taylor tractor of four cylinders. It was a huge machine too, with very high rear wheels. It, too, had a long roof, not quite full length, for this gently curved wooden covering only extended to the radiator, which looked more like a water boiler on a steam engine than a radiator. Orville's rig seemed a bit more lively, at least the separator gulped bundles faster than Adolph's, or seemed to, and blew out a greater volume of straw from its blower. It was not the machine to pitch bundles into. You had to work too hard.

When I was a kid, threshing was the highlight of the season on the farm. It was a social event as well as a necessary farm operation. The farmers in the whole neighborhood were together for two or three weeks during which they ate like kings, sweated like galley slaves, cussed like troopers when the horses became frightened as they approached the threshing machine, and joked and laughed heartily over their pre-dinner beer.

Threshing was a grand time, especially for the young, and we who were children before threshing passed out of the picture retain some fond memories of those days. I am one of those who barely made that era. When I left for college, threshing rings, as they were called, were almost a thing of the past.

As a ragged urchin in overalls, the most awesome sight around Heron Lake for me was Nimmerfro's giant Hart Parr engine parading by our place pulling the big wooden Hummingbird threshing machine. The Hart Parr barked sharply a couple of times, and then while coasting on the momentum of the huge flywheel would spit and backfire sporadically. It fascinated me because it reminded me about the dragons I had read about in the storybooks. I doubt if Adolph ever got the valves properly seated in his engine so it wouldn't spit and backfire so much.

One time we were herding cows along a nearby country lane when Nimmerfro's rig came along moving over to the neighbors. The welfare of the cows was forgotten as brother Edgar and I clambered aboard the Hummingbird as it jolted by for a free ride to Schumachers', where another thousand bushels of golden grain were due to be threshed yet before sunset.

Preceding the threshing rig, which lumbered along at two to three miles per hour, a procession of bundle racks clattered on ahead to load up at the new field. Occasionally a couple of spirited drivers would stage their own private chariot race as they made the transit to the next farm. When I became old enough to commandeer a bundle wagon myself and had a team of fast horses up front, I challenged another driver now and then. On one such occasion I never arrived at the next farm. The horses and the undercarriage did, but I sat glumly on the rack, now on the ground after being sheared off the wheels by a telephone post to which we veered too closely.

However, before advancing to the bundle wagons we hauled grain to the elevator from the threshing machine. The last vehicle to leave the threshing machine at late vespers was the heavily loaded grain wagon and its driver. More than once on a summer's eve a triple box of barley upon which slumped a barefoot boy was silhouetted against a red western sky as the lad clicked listlessly at the team of tired horses plodding slowly down the road to the Farmers Cooperative Elevator. I was sadly contemplating having to eat leftovers again from a grand thresher feast long since concluded. It seemed I always got hooked to haul that last load of the day.

The romance of threshing ended somewhat for me when I, to earn a little money, hired out as a bundle wagon driver. It was hard enough work to load bundles until they towered above into the sky (only a piker would draw up to the machine without a maximum load), but to have to pitch them into a ravenous threshing machine at a furious pace to keep the feeder full caused enough sweat to pour out of my pores to irrigate a strawberry patch. And I hate to sweat.

I figured there must be an easier way to make a living, such as gently spraying water on pretty flowers while standing in the shade on a hot summer day, like Father Jostock used to do. And so a budding vocation to the priesthood might have been given an impetus when we were pitching bundles on Joe Hullerman's farm one scorching afternoon.

Be that as it may, the sight of a blower belching straw and chaff over the top of a graceful strawpile and everything associated with it always brought joy to my heart. Regretfully, that scene has disappeared from rural America.

CHAPTER XXX

Farmerettes at Harvest Time

Mrs. Francis Knott of Dundee, Minnesota, upon reading my newspaper column on shocking grain, was prompted to write telling about life on the farm in those days for the girls and wives. I've paraphrased Mrs. Knott's lengthy and most interesting letter here.

The day began at 5 A.M. on their half section farm seven miles northeast of Dundee. Her dad yodeled the "good word" from the bottom of the stairs that it was time to get up. After he had let the 15 or 16 cows into the barn, you'd better be there with the milk pail or he wouldn't be in a good mood at all. I know what he means. I can still hear that guttural "dumpt" emitting from Pop's throat.

After the milking was done by hand, she carried the milk to the basement of the house, cranked the separator, and carried it back to the barns to feed the calves and pigs.

By this time her mother had breakfast ready, and, having worked hard for one and a half hours already, all ate heartily.

While dad and brother got the horses ready for the binder, the two girls had to feed some 600 young chickens, plus 40 or 50 ducks. "How I used to swear at those ducks," she says, "Their watering vessels were always so filthy with mud."

Next came the washing of the separator and milk pails, "another messy job." In addition, the cream had to be put down into the cooling tank by the well.

Water was pumped by the windmill, something else which has disappeared from the farm landscape. It ran all day when the wind blew in order to pump sufficient water for all the livestock. When the wind didn't blow, the girls started the little one cylinder engine and flipped the belt on the pulley to drive the pump. The belt slipped a lot, so they put some syrup on it, which solved the problem, although her dad didn't think much of the remedy. Girls weren't always so "dumb" when it came to mechanics.

Now it was time to go out to the fields and shock up grain behind the binder. They wore coveralls and straw hats so they wouldn't get so tan. Their mother always told them not to expose their face and arms to the sun "because you will begin to look old fast enough without the sun drying out your skin." Mrs. Knott observes: "Now the young chicks lay on the beach from May to September to get a tan, and we practically died from heat with that coverall buttoned up tight." In addition, they wore heavy gloves and stockings so their legs wouldn't get scratched. They didn't manage to keep up with the binder either, especially after 1934 when they got their first tractor.

After shocking grain all day until 5:30 P.M., they went in to do the chores alone while the men on the tractor and binder kept cutting until 8:00 P.M., when the grain got too tough with dew to continue. As much had to be cut on one day as possible, for "it might rain tomorrow."

By the time the men came in the girls had the chores all done. After the late supper, all they could think about was bed. But first they had to light the old kerosene stove and heat up some water for a bath.

Finally, the grain was cut and shocked, and there should be a few days rest? Nope. In the big garden were beans ready to be canned, and apples from the orchard, likewise. The "harvest apples" were made into apple sauce and apple butter.

In a few days the threshing ring went into action, and even before the telephone rang announcing the threshermen's meeting, mother and the girls were busily churning butter and baking cookies to get ahead a bit in preparation for the big days when the rig arrived at their farm, and then they would have to prepare a mountain of other food. The temperature stood at 90, and the old cook stove was going full blast browning bushels of cookies. The kitchen was so hot, the crickets moved out.

Then the great day came when the threshing rig moved into

the cow lot back of the barn, the big Hart Parr or Rumley engine hissing and barking like a dragon and scaring the chickens.

How many to feed three times a day, plus mid-morning and mid-afternoon lunch? Twelve bundle pitchers plus two "spike" pitchers, three grain haulers, and two thresher crewmen.

Up at four A.M. to quickly milk the cows and finish other chores before helping mother get breakfast for the two thresher crewmen who had left word the night before that they expected it at six A.M. "My sister and I always wondered why they couldn't eat breakfast at home."

Right after breakfast, stoke up the kitchen range for baking pies and browning the roast. Then out to the garden to dig up two or three bushels of potatoes by hand in the hot sun. Back into the house to make sandwiches and coffee for mid-morning lunch. Clean vegetables for dinner. "I was the youngest, so it was my job to do all the running. I bet I would make 40 trips a day to the cooling tank by the well where we had a ten gallon crock containing milk, cream, butter, cold meats." Refrigerators? Never heard of them.

At 11:30 A.M. the first two bundle haulers strode in, dirtied the clean towels, and sat down at table. It was 1:30 P.M. by the time the cooks could eat. Then hurry and do the dishes and make afternoon lunch. Hurry back to start supper, and then get the cows in for milking. "Have you ever tried to chase cows past a threshing machine?" she asks.

At long last the cows would be in their stanchions nervously chewing their cuds while the engine exploded away outside. The barn doors would be shut up tight to keep out the flies and keep the fly spray inside, but one never knew if it was the heat or the spray which killed the flies. "We would put something over our heads so our hair wouldn't smell like fly spray, put on our coveralls again, sit down and start milking. If some of these young girls today would have to do that now, they'd collapse in the gutter and stay there," Mrs. Knott observes.

Chores are only half done, but they'd have to go back into the house to get cleaned up and start serving supper for eighteen hungry men. The girls would rather enjoy serving these meals because there were a few young swains around who liked to kid them and flirt a bit.

By the time the dishes were done, it was almost 11 P.M. In bed upstairs it was so hot, sleep didn't come till 2 A.M. At the crack of dawn, up again for a repeat performance.

CHAPTER XXXI

Stack Threshing

Remember the days of stack threshing? Of course you do. That's why you like to take in a threshing festival somewhere in the fall each year to watch them do it again. The threshing machines, especially the old wooden ones, are about as rare now as the Atwater Kent radio. A few years ago you might still spot an old mill belching straw over a smooth strawpile on a rare farm here or there, but now it seems you have to go to one of these threshing shows to see one.

As I grew up on the farm, there was always some stack threshing done. There were always a few farmers who didn't want to join a threshing ring for shock threshing, and the threshing operators didn't object because they'd have some business yet durin the early fall. In fact, I heard the folks tell about threshing going on clear after Thanksgiving when the rigs were so scarce many farmers had to stack up their grain by necessity.

In the late twenties and early thirties we stack threshed most of the time, because Pa was quite an expert stacker. To stack up grain bundles properly required a certain technique. The middle would have to be kept high so the bundles on the outside rings would be slanting downward to shed the rain; a properly erected stack was a work of art. The circumference of the circular stack would be smaller at the base. Then it would be built outward up to four or five feet high. From then on it would gradually taper to a point twelve or fifteen feet high. The pivot bundle on the top would be anchored with a pointed lath driven downwards into the completed stack.

Properly erected, a stack of grain would weather over a year without harming the grain. Improperly done, the stack might start to settle off center and have to be threshed before the rains came or there would be nothing but a mess of wet straw. Occasionally one would see stacks like that here and there around the countryside, and the tell-tale sign that something was awry was a mess of green growing up the stack. Moisture got inside, you see, and the grain sprouted.

We usually got our grain stacked and the fall plowing done before school started. That way Pop got maximum service out of his two lads when they weren't wrecking stuff.

For example: One day after we had moved to the "villa" near Chatfield, Edgar and I had piled on a high top-heavy load of bundles in the field on top of the hill to bring down and stack by the barn. The dinner bell rang down in the valley where the farmstead was. I was hungry and suggested to Edgar we take the short cut down. This trail canted sharply at one point, but I assured him that if we rounded the bend fast enough we could make it without tipping over. He protested the proposed maneuver from his perch on top of the load, but I was in command up front with the reins in my hands, and I elected to whip the horses into a trot, and down and around the steep curve we went. You guessed it; we tipped over. In the scattered mess there was no sign of Edgar. Eventually, I saw a bundle wiggle and out of the spilled pile of bundles he emerged, spitting straw and angry epithets. He was extremely unhappy.

In the old days, after the shock threshing was completed, the two big rigs around Heron Lake, Orville Peterson's and Adolph Nimmerfro's, would begin stack threshing. With two or three men pitching off each stack, they'd mow them down pretty fast. I remember poking along on my way home from school one balmy September afternoon and looking up toward the west to see all of Frank Just's or Ignatz Filler's stacks had been converted into strawpiles during the day. Orville Peterson's huge old Aultmann Taylor was barking along smoothly as it powered his neat 36-inch Red River Special and was devouring the last of the bundles and spitting straw in a thick stream out over the top of a towering strawpile.

The Rotter Sisters out north of town had the neatest looking grain stacks every year. I remember, too, seeing a double row of eight stacks in Joe Pelzel's farmyard and was puzzled as to how they could all be threshed without moving the machine several times. I was told that it wasn't the machine which was moved but the stacks. Nimmerfro would shove the stacks up to the feeder with his huge old Hart Parr. The way the old monster snorted around and spit sparks from its exhaust stack, it's a wonder he didn't ignite the stacks.

One year we had such a bumper crop that we had 36 stacks of grain and that year oats were worth about ten cents a bushel. Wouldn't you know it!

Some farmers swore by stack threshing. They said the grain was cured better that way. They would talk about the stacks going into a "sweat," and after that when you threshed them you'd have golden grain the like of which would gladden the heart of any miller. I suspect, however, that it didn't gladden the heart of the farmer much when he saw what price it brought at the elevator.

Threshing as it's done today? This past summer we saw a gleaming new $20,000 combine lapping up a thick windrow of golden straw. In the air-conditioned cab sat a farmer listening to music as the machine hummed long. Was he happy? Naw, he was complaining how heavily mortgaged the machine was. In the days of stack threshing the only thing which was mortgaged was the farm.

At any rate, small grain is going out in this part of the country. Now its beans and corn, especially corn. Year after year it's corn on the same plot of ground. The soil is heavily fertilized, chemical sprays are applied, and I wonder if Mother Nature agrees with that kind of agriculture.

CHAPTER XXXII

A Study of Mules

It is early August on our quarter section farm in the mid-thirties. We had cut, shocked and stacked approximately eighty acres of small grain. Now the broad expanse of golden stubble was broken by clusters of four to six stacks of grain looking like brown castle turrets on the prairie. After these stacks had gone through their "sweat" for three or four weeks they would be ready for the threshing machine. Old timers said nothing threshed as beautifully and swiftly as these cured stacks of grain.

Once the grain was stacked, plowing would commence. And who was "it" to sit on a gang plow behind the horses for three weeks before school started, turning over eighty acres of stubble? It wasn't Pop when he had a couple of urchins around to be kept busy.

However, we had a couple of days of vacation while he got the plow lays sharpened at the blacksmith shop and dinged around the plow to get it ready. During this time we could watch the parade of grain wagons going by the place, hauling golden grain to the elevators in town. Shock threshing wasn't quite finished yet, and most farmers threshed directly from the shock instead of stacking their grain.

Many remember these old triple box grain wagons drawn by a team of horses. The driver sat on a plank laid across the top or sometimes he possessed a special spring seat mounted up there. When we hauled grain we had to sit on the hard plank.

Although some of the newer wagons had steel wheels, most of them were fitted out with thick wooden wheels with steel rims. As the summer progressed the wood dried out and contracted, and you were liable to lose a "tire," which the steel rim was called. Then you fastened it back on with wire until you found time to soak up the wood in a tray of used crankcase oil to cause the wood to swell again tightly against the steel rim.

While you had the wheel off you'd smear some black grease on the axle.

There was a certain amount of play between the wheel and axle, and under load, this play caused the wheels to "grunt" as it wavered between the inner and outer limits of its travel. So riding on a load of grain, the driver listened to a continual concert of throaty grunts from the wheels while he himself continually grunted at the horses, mostly from habit. The horses, swishing their tails around to drive off flies, strained against the load and paid no attention to the grunts of man or machine.

Since we live close to the town of Heron Lake, a procession of grunting grain wagons sort of funneled past our place, starting around eleven o'clock and continuing to dark. With these couple of days of vacations from the field, we'd try to determine where the threshing rigs were operating out in the hinterland by identifying the drivers of the wagons filing past.

There was one farmer, let's just call him John, who used mules almost exclusively, and these long-eared animals fascinated us mostly because you didn't see very many of them. And a mule acts quite differently than a horse under certain curcumstances. We had, for example, observed a frustrated farmer on occasion trying to get a team of mules to move when they decided that they weren't going to do so. The saying, "stubborn as a mule" was coined on fact, not fiction.

When Edgar and I noted John going by with a load of grain pulled by mules, we started discussing what a mule might do if you shot him in the ears with a BB gun. We decided to find out.

So we stood watch the next afternoon for the appearance of John with his mules. By and by, he came, and we hid behind the bridal wreath bushes by the road, our rather weak spring-driven BB guns in readiness. When the team of mules got within close range, we fired a salvo at their ears and managed to connect with the somewhat elusive targets.

The mules immediately stopped in their tracks, and the old gent couldn't get them to go again. Well, this performance on the part of the mules we had seen before. What would happen if they received a second pellet stinging them in the ears? If they took off again we would have discoverd an effective way to deal with stubborn mules. So, click, click, a second salvo was launched. Upon receipt of stumuli number two, what did they do? They started backing up.

Now this is a mighty awkward situation for a driver to have to contend with—going backward with a load of grain. John was clearly frustrated at the turn of events. His facial contortions revealed a set of pearly white teeth contrasting to his weekly growth of coal black beard.

You can't back up a wagon for long before it veers in one direction or another, and before you could sing out the first verse of Psalm 15 the load of grain had been backed into a shallow ditch whereupon the mules stopped again. But before you could sing out the second verse, the unpredictable creatures suddenly threw themselves into their collars and with a tremendous burst of energy, pulled the load right back up on the road as if nothing had happened. John wiped his brow with his red bandanna handkerchief and settled down for the remainder of the trip to the elevator, mumbling at his mules, and I suspect he wasn't flattering them much.

The moral is: idleness is the devil's workshop. Even two days of inactivity between grain stacking and plowing was not a healthy interval for two farm lads far too young to intelligently conduct research on mule behaviorism.

Some day I hope to meet up with John in heaven and explain the puzzling events of that afternoon as well as apologize for causing him a few moments of anxiety.

Autumn on the Farm

CHAPTER XXXIII

Husking Corn

We write for you farmers who are about to retire and are anticipating your social security checks while eyeing your expensive picker-sheller and wondering how much it will bring at an auction. Also for those who have already retired, to give them a moment of pleasant memories to replace those dark thoughts about the country going to the dogs and for farmers fifty years old or more who were out in the fields bulldozing through cornfields until midnight trying to get the crop in before the first big snow, so that by reading this, they might contrast the past with the present. And finally, for all those in the city who were once on the farm and who appreciate a bit of nostalgia.

Let's move you back to the year 1932, 11:30 A.M. on November 3. Since seven o'clock you've been darting back and forth between the two rows of corn, briskly husking and firing ears of corn against a wagon bangboard. The wind is raw, the temperature is 22 degrees, and a few flakes of snow are drifting down. But you're not cold. The fast pace of husking corn keeps you warm.

The wagon box is full now. There are almost 50 bushels in that load, and there will be another 50 bushels picked this afternoon. Anybody who can husk a 100 bushels of corn a day is considered a good cornhusker.

You didn't get out very early yesterday, though, because it was All Souls Day, and you took the kids to the first two Masses offered before school started. This is the day when the priest offered three Masses for the souls of the departed each year. And you told the kids that anytime you take time off to go to church, angels come out and help make up the time lost. But deep down in your heart, you don't believe it. Well, doggone it, maybe I am a hypocrite, but I hope the kids never discover it. They're a happy bunch, those kids. Haven't had a nickel in their pockets from one week to another, but they sure can laugh a lot.

The horses snap at half developed ears left on the stalks for the cattle, and sometimes you have to yell and swear at those horses so they keep the wagon abreast of you. Pheasant roosters dart back and forth in front of you. They are very plentiful. You note that it isn't far anymore to the end of the corn row, so you remove the shotgun from its brackets on the side of the wagon, insert a couple of shells into the double barrels, and start running for the end of the row. This scares the birds up, and you fire away. Two colorful roosters drop. These plus the two you got while slurping a tin of hot coffee from the thermos during mid-morning break will provide sufficient meat for supper. No other meat is left in the larder since it's still too early to butcher because the meat won't stay frozen quite yet. And Ma says we gotta save the rest of the hens for winter laying.

You pay no attention to the pheasant season. You figure as long as you feed the birds all year you're entitled to eat as many as you need for yourself and the family. But you shoot only as many as you need for food. You don't slaughter them for the fun of shooting them like some of those city folk do, and then leave them lying in the fields.

Yesterday a flight of Canadian geese settled in the cornfield to feed, and you shot one for Thanksgiving, hoping somehow you can preserve it until then. Turkeys? Nobody around raises them, and you don't have money to buy one. Neither does anyone else in the country, I guess, except the international bankers. You are fond of listening to Father Charles E. Coughlin of Royal Oak, Michigan, taking them apart in his Sunday radio talks.

You pulled into the yard with your load at noon and drove up along the hogyard fence and shoveled off a few bushels to your fattening Hampshires. Why you even feed them, you wonder sometimes. By the time you pay the trucker to get them to South St. Paul, there's hardly anything left of the check.

The rest of the load you shovel into the corncrib. It's narrow enough so that the corn dries out well during the winter. Then part of it is ground up for the chickens, and the rest goes to the hogs. Well, a little bit is ground up into corn meal for breakfast food. The hungry kids don't seem to notice the difference between that and the "boughten" breakfast food, and thrive on the home ground stuff. Also a couple of times a week you get served corn meal for supper in the form of "Johnny cake" which with that thin frosting on top is dern good.

As you unload the corn into the crib by hand, you can feel the little crimp in your back yet. You got that by pushing the backhouse into position again after Halloween when every one of those meditation parlors was tipped over. You figure maybe the kids have to have some fun once in a while. However, it was a bit nasty of them to upset George Muhler's at a time when he was inside it. The old man cussed such a blue streak his wife said he singed her curtains. The village cop was mad as blazes too. The kids had lured him into the swamp east of town on Halloween night with the call that there was a dead man found out there. While he was beating around among the cattails, they proceeded to let the air out of his tires, and took off to fill up Main Street with machinery from the implement company lots. That's not all they did. Because the editor of the village paper had severely warned them that no more tomfoolery was going to be tolerated this Halloween in a rather inflammatory article, they filled his stairwell with manure. The next morning he couldn't get down to his newspaper office to scorch them with another article until the fertilizer had been removed.

That full morning of vigorous cornhusking gave you a ravenous appetite. The big meal of the day in the winter comes in the evening when all the kids are home from school. For lunch your wife serves you a big bowl of piping hot nourishing soup. It was made from a half dozen different kinds of vegetable bits from the cellar storage bins plus a couple of bones left over from the roast. In those hard times the dog didn't get a bone until it had been cooked out first. In addition, there were a few slabs of ham from the depleting stocks in the smokehouse. These were served on thick slices of coarse whole wheat bread, and the repast was completed with a dish of home canned tomato sauce and a cup of coffee.

Your wife said something about grinding up some more winter

wheat into flour that she will need to bake again on Saturday. You make a note to take a sack from the granary to the elevator in town where they have a powerful hammer mill capable of grinding it up fine enough for flour. Your disk mill out in the granary can't do the job, and your single banger Waterloo stationary engine almost poops out when you throw the belt on to grind oats for hog meal.

One thing you learned about living on a farm, it's pretty hard to starve to death there even in the worst of times.

The wife also said we should take the kids to the parish bazaar tonight and give them a quarter to have a good time. The bazaar is a three-day affair. Half of the large church basement is blocked off for serving dinners every day, and the other half is a big carnival. The enterprising pastor is trying to make the interest on the debt and get a little ahead to buy the first carload of coal for the winter. When you have a cathedral for a church, and a leaky school and rectory, you need so much coal it's cheaper to buy it by the carload.

One time a carload of coal came in, and the pastor didn't have enough money to pay for it so they wouldn't let him unload it. The next Sunday he got up and scorched the brethren good. Told 'em that if they didn't stop hoarding their gold they could freeze to death on Sundays during Mass. Everybody looked at each other as if to say, "Who's got any gold?"

At the bazaar the pastor stretched the law a bit, installed a big roulette wheel and several slot machines. However, they were tampered with so they wouldn't cough up a jackpot. But one of the machines fooled him and coughed them up anyway. So he watched it very carefully, and when he figured it was about to "blow," he waded in and started playing it himself to keep the loot in the parish.

You laugh, and that brings you out of your reverie again as you sit in your living room in 1973 awaiting word from the wife that lunch is ready. The neighbor is tinkering with his snowmobile, and the thing sounds like a string of firecrackers exploding. You softly cuss as you think of what you are going to have to put up with the next few months of winter with that racket. It appears to you that people are getting mighty hard up for diversion in 1973 to spend a thousand dollars for one of those noisy gimmicks with which to aimlessly tear around the countryside looking for something to give them satisfaction. Of course, they never learned to enjoy books or music, never developed a satisfying hobby, are too lazy to develop skill on skis. Some can't bear the quiet of ski touring through the woods to observe nature in the winter. They must have something with power and speed. Feeling so inadequate in life's daily battles, at least they can have a sense of power on a contraption. But always they must be sitting on their asses. They can't bear exercise although on one of those contraptions they get their liver shook up plenty. One minute they demand a silkly smooth ride in a luxurious automobile which set them back four thousand dollars and the next minute they are out freezing to death aboard one of these gimmicks getting their gizzards shook up good. Man is a strange creature.

You sink back into reverie again and smile as you recall how the parishioners howled with pain every year when the assessments for pew rent came out, yet neither then nor now have Catholics ever really been hurt in the least by what they gave to the Church. Generally speaking, the Protestants have always outdone us in that department.

Your wife flips on the TV for the noon news, and soon your thoughts are back again to that bleak November day during corn picking and you completely ignore the TV.

You recall that while eating your lunch then you used to listen to the news on the new console Majestic radio which you managed to buy after trapping muskrats down by the lake bottom for a couple of years. The radio was advertised to have ten tubes, and that was considered the very ultimate in radios. The more tubes they had the better they were. But eventually you found out that five of the ten tubes were duds—just stuck in there for show to fool the customers. It was when one of the kids swapped a couple of weasel hides for an old three tube radio, took it down to shop class in school and dinged it up with the help of the instructor, brought it home, and it worked just as good as the ten tube job that you began to have doubts about advertising claims.

Things haven't changed. In 1973 they are fooling people just as much on TV, and actually convincing so many that happiness can come out of a bottle.

You used to listen to the noon news from WNAX, Yankton, S. D. It had almost as much power as that booming bootleg station XERA operating across the border from Del Rio, Texas, which harangued the gospel message every night, but most of the time was selling quack drugs.

On WNAX Chan Gurney was trying to convince the South Dakota farmers to buy Chinese elms from his Gurney Seed and Nursery Co. Said they were the only tree hardy enough to stand the droughts to form badly needed windbreaks before the whole state blew away.

After the news you relaxed for fifteen minutes listening to the Rosebud Kids wailing Country Western or, on alternate days, to a German hayseed from North Dakota by the name of Lawrence Welk and his oompah beat. The people like him because he didn't put on any airs and pretend he was a city slicker. When he talked he sounded like all the other krauts in the neighborhood.

In the distance you hear the guns starting up again by the lake, slaughtering some more ducks. The rich city people have fancy hunting lodges by the lake and most of the hunting rights. You figure that some day there won't be any ducks or pheasants left for the city folks to shoot, and then they will start shooting each other.

You don't like the idea of going to the bazaar because you want to stay home and listen to the politicians cussing each other over the radio. Big election coming up shortly. Opposing Herbert Hoover was a "smart aleck Yankee" by the name of Franklin Delano Roosevelt, and the Republicans called him that hoping to win votes away from him in the South. You figure that people suffering in the Depression are so fed up with Hoover, they'd vote for Barney Google if he ran.

It's snowing a little heavier as you go back to the cornfield after lunch. You've got twenty acres left to pick, and there could be a blizzard raging before you get done around Thanksgiving. And on top of that you still have to lay in a winter supply of wood since you can't afford to buy coal. Those cottonwoods by the creek aren't the best fuel for the heater, but that's all you've got. One farmer has a small stand of walnuts in his grove, and he's cutting them for firewood. The damn fool doesn't realize those trees are worth good money for making furniture.

CHAPTER XXXIV

I Hated Cornhusking

Today as I gaze across the valley from the study window of our rectory, perched atop "Soybean Slopes," we see the strip-cropped fields of amber corn awaiting the machines. I am reminded of those dismal Saturdays in October and November when I had to approach a field of corn to begin husking by hand.

The creaking old wagon with its swaying bangboard, against which the corn was thrown, would come to a halt at the beginning of the row, and the horses would immediately begin to feed on corn stalks or maybe an ear overlooked on a previous round. We'd hop off the wagon feeling like a convict at a stonepile.

Usually a chill wind pierced the frayed jacket tucked inside our overalls, and the only way to keep warm was to husk like mad. That involved a technique we never did master. A small husking hook was strapped to the inside of the wrist, and the idea was to rip into the husks of the ear of corn with it while simultaneously snapping off the golden ear with the other hand. That was supposed to require but a split second. For me it seemed to take a half hour.

A good cornhusker would go charging down the row snapping and throwing ears of corn at the bangboard in a steady barrage while at the same time bellowing and cussing at the horses to keep up with him. The temperature could be almost zero, and he would still perspire. But me? I felt like I was almost freezing to death every minute we were out in that field.

Eventually, I'd get an ear snapped off and thrown into the wagon, and then I'd stop and look around a bit. I'd note the V-formations of ducks and geese flying south, the little nuthatches, or whatever they were, flitting from stalk to stalk. Or maybe I'd see a pheasant running down the row ahead of us and would fire an ear at it to hear the squeaking noise it made when it took off in flight. Had I been allowed to bring a shotgun along, I would have been picking no corn at all. Remember how thick the pheasants were in those days?

Everything was against cornhusking as far as we were concerned. It was too cold. The corn rows seemed absolutely endless. The Gophers under Bernie Bierman were beating every team they played, and we couldn't listen to the games. The flights of pheasants, wild ducks and geese fascinated us. The box just never filled up so we could go home. And when Pa was around husking with us he grumbled and growled at us as much as he did at the horses—for good reason. Occasionally, Pa would hire a deaf and dumb man from the village to take his place with us. He did most of the husking—90 percent of it—and didn't make a sound, of course, and so we were spared having to listen to what a lousy cornhusker we were, a truth we would never argue about in the first place with anybody.

In the middle thirties, not all boys went through high school. But for me, the prospect of having to pick corn six days a week would be enough to stay in school for a hundred years.

It was nearly dark when we arrived home with a heaping load of yellow corn, and it was in that period of our life that we learned to love those beautiful autumn sunsets. When that red glow in the west finally arrived, we'd gaze on it with some semblance of ecstasy not so much because of the beauty of the scene, however, but because it meant that we could go home pretty soon.

Upon arriving home after a three-mile haul during which we brooded about those new wonderful machines called cornpickers, we'd still have to unload the corn into the crib with scoopshovels. Fortunately some of it would usually go to the hogs being fattened for market, and then all you had to do was remove the endgate and let the corn cascade out while you blessed the Lord for providing the law of gravity.

Finally, off would come the frayed gloves as we stood by the warm cookstove in the kitchen and sniffed at the delicious food on the table. It was amazing how hungry we got from just standing around all day. The shivering must have absorbed a lot of energy, I guess.

We'd pop the gloves into the warming oven above the cook-stove, but when Ma found them there, she's raise the roof and throw them out onto the porch.

Our wrists would be scratched from the cornstalks, but we wouldn't be caught dead applying some feminine skin lotion. I notice today they advertise some stuff called Cornhuskers Lotion for male namby-pambies. I think it's disgusting how men buy cosmetics these days.

Perhaps I hated to husk corn, but that was only one job on the farm. I still maintain farming is a fine way of life, a kind of life future generations will never know if the family farm goes down the drain or becomes too technical.

CHAPTER XXXV

Corn Shocks

You farmers who matured gracefully on God's green acres appreciate the finer things of life and enjoy rural rhapsodies of days gone by. Let us now serve up some fall scenes on the farm of those days.

As we write the maples hereabouts are turning gold and red. The robins have fueled up and have taken off for Yucatan or wherever they go for the winter. The Canadian snow geese are due to arrive any day to take up winter residence at the artificially heated Silver Lake in Rochester. Hot water from the power plant keeps it from freezing all winter.

'Tis autumn. And once upon a time we used to cut and shock up a little corn in this season.

Some remember a machine called a corn binder. One never sees them anymore—not even rusting away in a grove or thicket. They looked something like a single row corn picker with its rear end chopped off. When fall came, corn binders were used to cut cornstalks and tie them into bundles. These bundles were stood up into corn shocks. When we were ordered out to shock corn bundles the first time, the bundles were taller than we were, and trying to maneuver these bundles into a shock was like trying to dance the waltz with an adult who had wooden legs.

Silos weren't as numerous in the middle thirties as they are now, but those farmers who had one also had a corn binder. After the corn had dried out to its proper level to make good silage, the corn shocks were loaded into a flat bed wagon and hauled to the silo, at the base of which was a silo filler. This machine swallowed the corn bundles, chopped them into cow salad, and heaved it up to the top of the silo through a blower pipe.

A silo filler made lots of noise. The racket came mostly from the large blower, which, when revved up, sounded like a cow mooing but holding the high note, and if somebody in the neighborhood was filling silo, the whole township upwind heard about it. While we didn't have a silo we cut some corn down and shocked it up for corn shredding.

A field of corn shocks you don't see anymore either, but they were very picturesque. Along about Halloween and Thanksgiving teachers in the elementary grades will paste up pictures of corn shocks on classroom windows, and you'll also see them in supermarket ads around Thanksgiving.

More than likely these pictures show pumpkins at the base of the shocks. However, the fact is that farmers didn't usually plant pumpkins in their cornfields. Our pumpkins were grown in the corner of the garden along with squash, cucumbers, and watermelons.

Farmers would harvest their pumpkins before Halloween or the town kids would come out and steal them to make jack-o-lanterns. That wasn't all they stole. They used to make a sport of raiding watermelon patches too, and the farmers had the courtesy to pump shotgun pellets over the tops of their fleeing figures instead of lodging a few in their posteriors. We figured most town kids weren't much good because all they did was get into mischief for lack of something to do while we had to work like coolies.

Pheasant roosters darted back and forth between the corn shocks and crawled inside of a shock to roost for the night. When the pheasant hunting season opened, the town folks came out and shot half of these pheasants without asking for permisson to hunt, and it made me mad. I wanted to shoot the hunters with my BB gun, but Pa said, "nothing doing."

There was another machine you don't see around anymore, and that was a corn shredder. It looked something like a small threshing machine. Mounted on the rear of it was a similar blower pipe out of which spewed shredded corn. For those not having silos, like us, a pile of shredded corn was deposited by the barn for winter fodder.

A corn shredder, like a silo filler, took lots of power. We hooked it up to the little Model B John Deere because that's all we had on the place to supply belt power except a single cylinder five h.p. engine used for cracking corn, but that noisy little popper would choke to death just running the shredder empty. The shredder was a heavy overload for the John Deere, but the plucky little snortfire wouldn't quit firing although the manifold got red hot, and the clutch was always slipping a little until it burned out. However, it didn't take long to slip in a new set of clutch facings inside the pulley once you got it cooled down enough to touch without setting the gloves on fire.

I suppose everyone carries vivid scenes of extraordinary beauty in their subconscious which they can flash before their mind's eye occasionally. This time of the year we can easily conjure up one such scene, namely, a field of corn shocks silhouetted against a red October sky after sunset. High above the shocks are several V-formations of wild ducks gliding to bleed off altitude as they head in toward the tall swamp grass of the shallow lake a mile or two to the east. The quiet evening air is broken by these arriving flotillas quacking their greetings to their friends below, already nesting in the water for the night.

CHAPTER XXXVI

Thanksgiving 1934

It was late fall in 1934. The nation was in the depth of the Great Depression. Thanksgiving had arrived, and like the Pilgrims, rural America gave thanks around tables loaded with good food, and like the Pilgrims, they raised all of it themselves on the land.

A bin in our basement was heaped with potatoes, potatoes which had grown a little bigger because we had gone down the rows and shook off those orange squirming potato bugs every other week in the summer. And while thus engaged, who could resist slipping one or two of these choice creatures down sister Toots' neck, and the ensuing commotion was tantamount to the rebels firing on Fort Sumter. I had to hide out for a spell until the wrath of the honorable ancestors cooled a bit.

Next to this bin was another full of carrots, pumpkins, squash, and some cabbage heads, while the walls of the subterranean food treasure were lined with shelves of home-canned tomatoes, beans, ground cherries, and apples—products of much labor over a hot stove in August.

No doubt it was the same in your basements too. Remember?

In the other corner of the basement by the cream separator was a five gallon can full of rich cream. In preparation for the holidays especially, we had to stand by the hour thumping the stuff into butter with the wooden handle of the churn. The one who caused the most commotion around the house got that job even though he protested that he needed to finish his library book in order to improve his mind. Every time I see neatly packaged pounds of butter in the stores today, I am still reminded of how I repented for my sins.

A case or two of fresh eggs was stored down there too. They were worth less than a penny apiece at the store. But no matter, they tasted good when fried with some of that smoked sausage hanging in rows on poles out in the tile smokehouse.

Out in the pigpen stood a hundred or so fat white Hampshires. Before the holidays a couple of them were to become victims of a bloody sacrifice under the box elder tree, to provide ham and bacon plus some sausage.

The rest of the hogs we gave away to Armour's or Swift's for three cents a pound. That covered the trucking costs and gave us about two cents an hour for our labor. However, Armour's and Swift's didn't fall into the spirit of the season and give any meat away.

On Thanksgiving Day the farmers told the Lord they were glad to give away their hogs, but after they got home from church they resumed their old habits and griped like the devil about it.

The hen house was full of White Rock hens and fat roosters. When company was coming and the order came out of the kitchen, I moved out to snare one of those proud chanticleers with a long leg hook and deprived him of his colorful head on the wood chopping block. Finally, when the ranks of the roosters had been thinned out a bit there wasn't so much racket at dawn anymore.

Turkeys we didn't have. We got the impression in school that they were supposed to be running wild in the woods because we always saw pictures of the Pilgrims with muskets loping after them through the woods. So, once before Thanksgiving we took the BB gun and went out to the grove to get one. Meanwhile, Toots enquired from Pa whether there were wild turkeys around, and he said not in the whole state. She came out to the woods and whinnied something awful at me for which she got nicked with a pellet in the posterior. That time I really had to hide out for a long time.

By Thanksgiving cornpicking was done, and the cribs were full. What was left over was thrown on the ground for the hogs to eat and fatten up on, so we could give them away when they were heavy enough.

President Roosevelt told the farmers they shouldn't give away their hogs like that. Raise less of them, he says, so the city people would get hungry enough to pay for them. Well, they were hungry enough as it was. In fact, some of them were starving. So he dished out loads of WPA money to them, but the packers kept all the money for the meat, and the farmers still gave away all their hogs.

Then he hatched a scheme whereby the farmers were supposed to kill their little pigs, and he'd give them a few nickels if they did. But the farmers hated to waste anything even though the government was setting a wonderful example at that sort of thing. So the little pigs just grew up to become big pigs like the politicians.

Now some say we have too many people as well as too many pigs. So what do we do? We proceed to kill the people before they are born while the little pigs get off scot free.

After the pigs finished eating the corn off the cobs we members of the new generation had to go out and pick up the cobs to burn in the cookstove, since we didn't have money to buy coal. If any kid started whining, "There ain't nothin' for kids to do in this burg," he was sent out to pick cobs, and the problem was quickly solved. By the way, there was a generation gap in 1934, but not very wide—just the length of a razor strap.

So Thanksgiving 1934 was a grand affair. There was plenty of good food, and it didn't cost anything but the sweat of our brows. Christmas was a wonderful time too on the land, and we have a special chapter on that.

Perhaps God was blessing us because we always gave away our hogs.

Wintertime on the Farm

CHAPTER XXXVII

A Winter Day on the Farm

We present a day in the life of a farm boy during mid-winter before the era of the Great Inflation and GNW (gross national waste).

It is Saturday morning. You sleep a half hour later since there is no school. You are supposed to get up at 7 A.M., but it is so cold in the bedroom it takes a half hour to work up enough courage to throw off the heavy quilts. It is about 22 below outside, and about 22 above inside the bedroom upstairs. The frost is half an inch thick on the single windowpane, so you can't see if a blizzard is commencing or not. You hope there is because then you won't have to work so hard that day. The frost is so thick on the windows because there are no storm windows on the east and south sides of the house. Pop can afford to put them only on the sides where the wind howls the most.

You stand in your long underwear and try to break the ice in the wash basin, but you usually end up running downstairs right away to huddle around the coal heater and forget about washing. Rising was usually preceded by a storm erupting from the throat of the Honorable Ancestor who has returned to the house because you haven't shown up in the barn after he has milked two cows already.

The small barn is heavily steamed inside due to inadequate ventilation, and the frost on the windows in an inch thick. It smells terrible in there, for Saturday barn cleaning, with the distribution of fresh, dry straw, has not yet been done.

The milk, of course, was not pasteurized, and we ingested a few million microbes and bacilli every day just from our breakfast milk served fresh and warm from the cow. We thrived on it, bacteria and all. Nobody ever got typhoid fever. Mumps, measles, chicken pox, pink-eye, and sore throat from having the tonsils taken out, but not typhoid. Every kid had his tonsils taken out because the doctor was getting hard up during the Depression, I guess.

Sometimes we kids would go down to watch old 403 come in. When she took off, the engineer always shot too much steam to the big drive wheels, and they'd spin on the rails once or twice, leaving burn marks on the rail.

Many times I decided to become an engineer and have some fun spinning wheels on take-off. Whenever I could get my hands on the old Chevy, I'd try to spin the back wheels too in taking off, but it would only do it on gravel or ice because the old clunk lacked power. That's because Pop would never take it in and have new spark plugs or points put in or have the valves ground. I notice the kids today like to spin the wheels of their dad's car on take-off, but they have more than enough power and do fearful things to the tires and transmissions besides making screeches like a dog when one steps on its paws by accident.

When the farmers built their cooperative creamery in the village, we hauled our cream there instead of putting it on old 403 for Lakeville. Maybe that's why old 403 eventually went out of business.

The government or somebody must have gotten after the creamery folks because they kept the place slick and clean. They were always squirting water on the floor all day, and the men who worked there always wore white overalls and reminded me a little of the doctor and nurses at the little hospital by the park. The farmers could track manure only as far as the office, where they watched their cream being tested before they went home.

It was a waste of time for the farmers to watch this testing, because they didn't know what was going on anyhow. The creamery man would put some red or green stuff on top of a sample of cream in a test tube, put the tube in a machine which whirled it around some and then took it out, looked at it, and marked something on a slip of paper. If he wanted to impress the farmer a little more because he figured the guy was a penny-pincher, he would put a pair of calipers to the test tube to measure something for greater accuracy. The farmer was usually duly impressed and satisfied.

I was always impressed too and decided to become a scientist, but when I asked Pa for a chemistry set he said "nothing doing" and grumbled something about blowing up the house. So a couple of weeks later when the undertaking parlor burned down on main street, I decided to become a fireman instead.

However, if these people at the creameries were cheating Pop and the other farmers by their fancy testing techniques, then they probably went to hell when they died. That's what they said in catechism class would happen to people who cheated. However, there didn't seem to be any crooks in town, so maybe they didn't cheat. In those days farmers figured the only crooks around in the country were the Democrats and the Wall Street bankers.

After the milking and separating were done, we could come in for breakfast. This consisted of stuff called "farina" along with some bacon and bread. Farina was winter wheat we ground in the mill uptown. You poured some warm milk on it, added some sugar, and it was pretty good stuff. The bacon, of course, was plentiful because we could butcher all the hogs we wanted since they brought so little on the market. The farmers cussed President Hoover a lot and were on the verge of becoming Democrats as the 1932 election came up.

On Saturday mornings in winter Edgar and I were assigned to clean out the chickenhouse while dad cleaned out the barn. This building housing the laying hens wasn't ventilated right or something because it always got awfully wet in there. Therefore, every Saturday we threw out the wet straw through a window onto a horsedrawn sleigh and scattered it out in the field. Sleigh riding wasn't anything new to us, and if the idea of a sleigh ride party doesn't make me jump up and down with joy today, it's because sleigh riding was always associated with work on the farm.

If we got into an argument while cleaning out the henhouse, we'd throw wet straw at each other. The hens penned up in the building were very much disturbed at the method of warfare used because they had to run for cover or get bashed by a clod of wet straw. They cackled a lot which brought Ma out of the house to see what was going on. She was very jealous of her hens because the eggs they laid bought our groceries—what few we bought.

During the depression chicken thieves were conducting nocturnal forays about the countryside, and one night they raided our chicken castle. Boots, our dog, happened to be home that night and gave the alarm.

Pa got out of bed at the canine alarm and fetched the shotgun from the garage. From there he had a good view of the chicken house and saw the rustlers emerge lugging sacks full of wriggling chickens. You see we had a yard light (we were close enough to the village to hook on to their "juice"). Pop warned them to drop the sacks and punctuated his demand with a blast from the old canon. They did and took off through the grove with Boots after them, picking at their heels. We were never bothered by chicken thieves again. The word got around. Too much light on the subject, a nasty dog, and a farmer who is quick to let fly with buckshot didn't add up for a successful heist.

While we were working outside all morning on Saturday, Ma and the girls were doing the housecleaning, including a thorough scrubbing of the floor.

Having expended considerable energy at this task, they were in no mood to tolerate any "tracking" by rubes who failed to remove their manure encrusted overshoes. But boys are not always conscious of the feminine viewpoint in this matter, and gnawing with hunger, we might barge in occasionally forgetting to remove the footgear. Hence, the girls always posted a guard by the kitchen door when the old clock on the bureau in the dining room threatened to clank away twelve times.

If you walked in with the overshoes still on, WHAM! down came a sturdy mop handle on your noggin. This direct procedure occasionally brought forth something reminiscent of the western ditty: "The stars at night shine big and bright, deep in the heart of Jackson County." It proved to be very effective pedagogy, however, and eventually the meridian dragoons could relax in the posting of the guard.

Noon dinner over, Pop listened to the 12:30 P.M. news by

Cedric Adams. He sat in his chair by the Majestic radio console while we minutely examined all the advertisements which came in by the morning mail. We were particularly interested in the ads appearing in the farm magazines featuring cars or tractors. Sometimes we'd approach the honorable progenitor with an ad for a new car and urge him to give it careful consideration. We soon learned not to approach him while he was listening intently to the noon news for then we'd be told in no uncertain terms to get lost. For one thing he didn't want to miss an item unfavorable to FDR (President Franklin D. Roosevelt), whom he called "a cocky bastard gettin' too big for his britches." At which Mama remonstrated with him for using vulgar language in front of the children.

CHAPTER XXXVIII

The Winter of 1935-36

We were beginning to think that the days of the old-fashioned severe winters of old were over, and then came the winter of 1969. It reminds us a bit of the winter of 1935-36 with its incessant snowfall. The only difference is that in early 1936 we had almost a month of steady below zero temperatures.

I was becoming a teen-ager then, only I didn't know it. You see, the term wasn't used then, so I remained in the human race, carrying out the duties of my state in life in a normal manner, and accepting life as it came with a fair degree of contentment. I knew I'd get my head knocked off if I didn't like how things were going and opened my yap too far.

The snow piled up on the roads, but the snowplows didn't get around to clearing them for a few days. Sometimes secondary roads waited weeks to get cleared. The worst snowdrifts had to be cut through with big lumbering caterpillars with a V-plow hung in front. A minimum of a week passed before the big cats arrived. The Omaha railroad passing through Heron Lake used a steam-driven rotary plow, the operation of which caused more excitement among the "kinder," as we kids were called, than the exploits of Apollo rockets today. The trains had to get through because small towns were more dependent on them for daily necessities than they are now. Mail came exclusively by train, and much of the cream was shipped via railroads.

In bad weather we went to school in horse-drawn sleighs. The sleigh with a crude box above the runners might have been used to haul manure the day before, and a fresh layer of straw in the box hardly masked the odor, but we weren't very "finicky." We weren't frightened to death by B.O., because nobody was trying to sell deodorants and making people so terribly sniff conscious.

If the snow got deeper than the horses' bellies, you simply

picked a trail across the windblown fields. You kept warm under heavy horse blankets, which were used primarily to cover the horses in bitter cold weather while they stood hitched to a post in town awaiting the pleasure of their masters. I can still see a line of teams under horse blankets standing in front of the church on Sundays. One didn't miss Mass on Sunday because of the weather.

School was seldom called off because of the weather either. Those living five or six miles out might find it too rough to buck snowdrifts all the way to town on some days, but school went on anyway. In fact, I think Sister was a bit relieved when the big boys didn't make it because they didn't behave so well in school all the time. During the noon hour they used to play a card game called "tarok," and that wasn't so bad except it was hard on the desk tops the way they used to bang their knuckles down on them when they came forth with a good card. However, when they took to bombarding kids coming out of the outside toilets with snowballs and beating up on little shrimps like me, that's when Sister became a bit distressed.

Occasionally old "Hedrick," the janitor, couldn't get the old boiler steamed up right, and we sat in our heavy clothes during class, but school went on just the same. In fact, the only time we got out of school was for a couple of hours occasionally when the firemen put out a roof fire resulting from a defective chimney. But that never occurred during the winter as there was usually too much snow on the shingles to prevent them from igniting.

During the long blizzardy evenings after the chores were done, we sat around and read books. Fortunately, we were spared some of the modern TV garbage. Or I practiced on the clarinet while Edgar made doleful sounds on his cornet to make the dog howl. This caused considerable static from the other kids, who were trying to do homework. We had to quit, though, if Pa wanted to hear some politicians bark or maybe listen to "Amos 'n Andy."

Trails to the outbuildings had to be scooped out with hand shovels after a big snowstorm. Once we even had to tunnel through a huge snowdrift to get to the henhouse. People didn't keel over from heart attacks shoveling snow. They were in magnificent shape physically from constant hard work.

The use of cars was severely limited during the winter. For one thing, the alcohol used as antifreeze boiled out so often. Secondly, you had to hand-crank them to get them started after building a fire under the crankcase, and sometimes that burned down the garage. In addition, the Model Ts or Model As were famous for "kicking;" that is, backfiring and spinning the crank in the opposite direction. This would break the arm of the cranker as cleanly as a whistle. See our chapter "The Model T in the Wintertime."

Life slowed down a bit during a severe winter, that's about all. People took severe weather in stride, and never had a thought of going to Florida. Who could afford it during the depression years? Rural people never worried about snowstorms coming because they didn't know they were coming. By the time we heard something about it on the radio it was half over. Weather forecasting isn't exactly always accurate in the seventies. In a recent March scores of peoples around here were marooned one night by a doozer of a blizzard which was forecast as "light snow."

In the thirties rural people grappled with life as they found it, winter or summer, and developed into tough, stalwart men and women.

CHAPTER XXXIX

Butchering a Hog

Along about early December the family meat larder was about empty of Ma's canned meat, and the smokehouse was shorn of sausages. The temperature was getting low enough to start butchering again.

The scene is now set for the following heart-rendering melodrama.

One wintry December Saturday we were engaged in our favorite pastime of devouring the contents of a library book in the corner of the "front room," as living rooms were called, when the Lord High Executioner of pork and beef and also my immediate honorable ancestor, appeared on the scene and demanded that I "get a move on" to help butcher a pig.

Deep dismay entered my soul. Such a messy business for a devotee of the fine arts like me! Where was our neighbor, Louie Winkler? He always helped Pop convert a squealing hog to banquet table fare.

But you didn't argue with said honorable ancestor if you didn't want to study astronomy in the middle of the day, so I put down **The Adventures of Huckleberry Finn** and reluctantly trudged out to the pigpen.

The Lord High Executioner was to regret having me as his chief assistant before that afternoon was out.

The victim for the sacrifice was grabbed at random from the herd of fat porkers enjoying a meal of corn on the cob. Pop got a vise-like grip on the animal's ears and was soon merrily dancing the ballet while trying to subdue the creature who by now was contributing quite an aria to the performance.

"Don't just stand there like a dumbbell! Grab him by the legs!" I could hardly hear the exasperated command over the pig's swelling solo.

We managed to edge the hog out of the pen in short stages while Pop began to sweat like . . . you guessed it.

During the struggle, my thoughts went clear back to Jerusalem, of all places. At a recent religion class, Father Boecker had told us how the Hebrew priests would slay hundreds of sheep and oxen in the Temple on big religious festivals and pour the blood around the altar as a gesture of propitiation for sin, etc. Boy, I'd never volunteer for that kind of priesthood, I thought. We're having enough trouble with just one victim whose blood was going to be made into blutwurst and not sprinkled around any altar.

As Pop reached for an instrument of destruction, I relaxed my grip momentarily, and the pig got loose. Now trying to catch a pig after he's got some running room, a two-acre potato patch to be exact, would be good practice for a high school tackle. But we didn't have a football team in our school then, so the pig was able to make quite a few touchdowns. Meanwhile Edgar was called off the bench, and the two of us worked up quite an appetite while the coach stood on the sidelines and cussed in German.

We finally cornered the puffing porker, and the Grand Surgeon moved in and performed a goiter operation on him. Pop was good at that. His surgery was enormously successful—his patients always promptly died. We hooked a horse to the victim and dragged him underneath a box elder tree for an autopsy.

Fortunately, my performance that afternoon got me fired permanently as the Lord High Executioner's chief assistant, and Louie was pressed back into service whenever the meat larder dwindled. I was transferred to the sausage making department. A few of my critics who think I put out a bunch of baloney once in a while now know where it all got started.

CHAPTER XL

The Model T in the Wintertime

I was a little cherub then, with runny nose and tangled hair, supposedly growing into the age of reason there on the Hartneck Place, and I was beginning to acquire certain powers of observation concerning the world about me. So, encased in an oversized sheepskin coat and red scarf wound around my noodle leaving space open for those darting and inquisitive eyes, I would stand and watch the proceedings when, on rare days in the wintertime, Pa decided he needed his Model T Ford to carry him on a mission somewhere. As we mentioned before, Pa had one of these "Tin Lizzies" of 1916 vintage.

Most of the farmers, if they had a car at all yet, had, like Pa, a Model T, Henry Ford's unique contribution to greater mobility for the nation. It was a practical conveyance, but not too practical in the winter months.

Here then is a blow-by-blow account of how a Model T was activated for a winter trip on a cold day.

The first step was to jack up a rear wheel to reduce friction in the cranking process. It was easier to spin the hind wheel along with the crankshaft than to fight the glue-like oil in the clutch housing. Next, the spark lever underneath the steering wheel was advanced, the gas lever nearby also advanced a bit, and the magneto switch turned on.

The driver, still full of enthusiasm and expectation, hopped out to the front of his machine, pulled the choke wire protruding from a hole in or around the radiator, grabbed the crank, and proceeded to spin it with a burst of energy, the revolving rear wheel acting now as a sort of flywheel.

At this point in the operation, disaster often struck—especially if the contraption undergoing the cranking was a Model T. The engine had a bad habit of "kicking" on the first explosion; that is, the first burp reversed the order of revolution and spun the crank handle back in the opposite direction to catch the arm or wrist of the pioneering winter driver. Presto! A neat and clean fracture of said appendage. Whereupon said driver would yowl with pain and retreat quickly to the warm sanctuary of the kitchen and yowl some more, resolving to reduce his once pride and joy to a heap of rubble with a maul once his cast was removed. Usually the wife was not of much comfort with her unsympathetic observation, "I told you to leave that car on blocks all winter. I didn't need it to go any place today."

Small town papers regularly reported arms fractured in the community throughout the winter when enterprising winter drivers got their kicks. And the local doctor found another source of income dropped into his lap—besides the old standby, taking out tonsils. These same small town journals also carried explicit instructions on the proper method of grasping a crank in order to avoid this needless destruction of cartilage and lime structure. Well, they still warn people today about the dangers on the highway and methods to counteract them, but the roadways still remain the most lethal hunks of real estate in the nation.

Pa, however, managed to outwit his Model T when she kicked, but he had still other problems with his horseless carriage. All too often the recalcitrant Tin Lizzie wouldn't even manifest enough life to inflict a kick. Thereupon, the dogged and determined driver (a "stubborn German" was the way Ma put it) who made up his mind he wasn't going to hitch up a team to a sleigh that day, strode, with dismay written all over his face, toward the kitchen stove to procure a tea kettle full of boiling water. This bubbling fluid, poured into the radiator, might serve to warm up the innards of the power plant sufficiently to effect some action therefrom. It wasn't wasted effort exactly because water would have to be poured into the radiator anyway after the clunk started. Antifreeze, as we know it, was nonexistent in those days. There was wood alcohol, but that tended to evaporate and disappear faster than Scotch whiskey at an old-fashioned Irish wake.

Another method of applying heat to the engine consisted of building a fire from corncobs beneath the crankcase. This had the distinct disadvantage of sometimes causing acute distress to the driver after he had waged a losing battle trying to put out a conflagration which destroyed both the car and the garage.

Although Pa used the corncob method on occasion, he was lucky enough to forestall the production of this kind of excessive heat.

But even after the four cylinder dream of Ford engineers proceeded to clatter unsteadily in the cold, the lot of the winter driver was not without further cares. As we said, he would then have to fill the radiator with water and drain it out again after returning his runabout to its roost. In the meantime, while in transit, he relied upon a horse blanket or fur robe draped over the hood and radiator to keep things from freezing while it was parked in front of the church, store, or local watering place. If he miscalculated the temperatures or forgot about his mechanical beast of burden sitting outside and being unmercifully attacked by Jack Frost's icy paws, he might discover to his chagrin on the way home that his radiator had frozen up. The water in the cylinder jackets would turn to steam and escape through the radiator cap sending up a plume of steam which clouded up the windshield. This, likely as not, tended to produce unhappy epithets from his lips and would bring on stern admonitions from his outraged wife reminding him not to contribute unworthy phrases to the vocabulary of the children present who by now were delighted at the phenomenon of the family auto turned into a steam locomotive.

Many times our Model T would have been left at peace to gather frost and sifted snow in the garage, and Pa might have been spared many frustrations, but Ma insisted on the use of the car. She expressed a distinct repugnance on occasion to riding in a sleigh since it served other manifold needs on the farm, one of which was hauling manure.

When on a frigid morning we suffer deep disappointment and diminution of pride because our Belchfire V-8 fails to fire up, we might think of the lot of the poor winter motorist in the middle and late twenties.

CHAPTER XLI

Christmastime in the Country

Christmas is a time people like to remember or anticipate. Older people are more inclined to remember.

The celebration of Christmas has changed a bit over the years. First of all, it wasn't rushed quite so much in earlier years. The stores weren't decorated until two weeks before Christmas, because it wasn't the commercial festival it is now. For one thing, people didn't have as much money to spend as they have today. Christmas shopping could be done at the last minute, more or less. Much of the merchandise was ordered via mail order catalogues.

Christmas trees were put up on the day before Christmas, and the decorations were mostly homemade—fancy cookies and candy canes were hung from the tree, which was interlaced with silver tinsel. And always a star glowed prominently from the top of the tree. Some may remember that Christmas candles instead of bulbs were used, and what a fire hazard that was!

The passenger trains coming through the village grew appreciably longer around Christmastime, with the addition of many more mail cars, since mail was hauled entirely by train. Locomotives were steam driven, and their eerie whistles echoed through the still starry nights over rural America.

Just before the Christmas holidays the kids would be doing their homework around the circular dining room table while the radio played softly. Then all of a sudden for the first time "Silent Night" would come over the air. Everybody would stop to listen, including mother, who was darning socks in her rocking chair. She would smile, and we all felt good inside. But there was no glut of Christmas music far in advance of Christmas Day, and people weren't tired of it by the time Christmas came.

Pre-Christmas parties were unknown, but there were plenty of them during the period between Christmas and New Year's.

In rural America these were neighborhood gatherings. The older folks played cards, and the children amused themselves around the premises playing their own games, but they eventually curled up and fell asleep on sofas and in the corners of the room before the party broke up. The younger children slept through the ride home in the sleigh under the clear winter sky as the sleigh runners crunched on the packed snow.

Softly falling snow on Christmas Eve forming a blanket of six inches or so—there have been Christmas Eves like that, though certainly quite rare of late in this climate.

Putting Christ back into Christmas was a slogan unknown when I was a kid. They didn't have to put Him back; He was always there. However, preachers did harangue about keeping St. John the Baptist in Advent, and anybody who did some merrymaking and carousing before Christmas was a heathen. Children had to be on their best behavior or St. Nick would leave them a stick. Advent was a period of quiet anticipation.

Santa Claus was rarely seen before Christmas anywhere, but he did show up often on Christmas Eve in many a home, and the eyes of children grew wide with awe while little hearts beat with a pace akin to that of a captured rabbit.

Such was the Christmas of yesteryear, and not too many years ago at that. But let's look specifically at Christmas of 1934.

In July 1934 it looked like we would be dried out for sure, and that Christmas of that year would be bleak indeed, but one Sunday night the rain came, and a good share of the crop was saved. Monday morning we were to start cutting the small grain for what hay we could salvage from it. Much of the Great Plains was a dust bowl that year, and even much of southern Minnesota were not so lucky as we in Jackson County. At least we had feed for the livestock, and the garden came through with the help of water trucked from Jack Creek and diligently dished out at the roots of the plants. We could have another good Christmas without money.

But hard up as we were, Christmas was in the air in the middle of December, and people smiled a bit more. In our town of Heron Lake, they hung a couple of rows of red lights across main street, and we thought they were very elegant. In Robson's store were a few toys and dolls in one corner, and we gazed at them with wide eyes. A coasting sled in the Briardale store is what we had our hearts set upon, but when we asked Ma what Santa Claus might bring that year, the answer was short and to the point: "A switch."

To get out of helping make sausage in the kitchen those winter evenings we wangled a small part in the Christmas operetta our pastor, Father Boecker, was cooking up for presentation in the City Hall (otherwise known as the Majestic Theatre, when they showed those new talking pictures once a week). It was also the setting for wedding dances where "moonshine" was brought in via pocket flasks and swigged in corners with silly grins. Eventually, the lusty lads now "lubricated" would start a fight. It happened at almost every one of these dances.

The climax of this operetta had the Three Kings coming down the middle aisle singing "We Three Kings of Orient Are" in deep bass voices. They followed the star which was pulled along on a wire ahead of them, and I was in charge of pulling that tinsel star along the "heavens." However, the star always got stuck on the wire, and tugging at it only tore it to pieces. Since I couldn't move the star across the sky, I was fired, and the final production featured the Kings finding their way to Bethlehem without a star. Besides, the eyes of all would be more centered on the Kings draped in those fancy quilts.

Santa Claus showed up at our house in 1934, mostly because Uncle "Butch" was in town for the holiday. On Christmas Eve he came trooping into our living room where we kids were huddled like scared rabbits. Well, I wasn't because I was too old to believe in Santa Claus. He proceeded to quiz the little kids in catechism before he reached into his sack for the present they were to get. They couldn't recite any catechism when they were scared to death. The sight of the switch in his sack didn't help matters. What they didn't know was that he didn't know any catechism himself, and they could have bluffed him so easily. As I recall that was the only year Santa Claus appeared in person. Other years he came down the chimney while we were sleeping, and we were glad to settle for that rather than a religious inquisition.

What did an urchin get for Christmas in those days? A pair of mittens, a pair of socks, a scarf maybe. Always a necessary item of clothing, not toys.

People were accustomed to make presents and send them off by parcel post. A jar of pickles, some preserves, a hand-knit scarf maybe, an apron, etc. Aunt Nora usually sent a quart of home-made wine which was really moonshine, colored a bit to disguise it. Her husband was a bootlegger.

As Christmas approached we liked to go down to the depot to meet the 2:40 P.M. train and watch the unloading of the increased volume of merchandise representing Christmas presents, and the greater than usual number of people getting off. They were coming home for the holidays, of course.

Christmas, centering around that first Christmas, started six in the morning. First there was always a big procession from the basement upstairs to the crib, and every altar boy got in on that parade, and, for a welcome change, got a chance to wear red cassocks.

What fascinated me was not what went on upstairs later, but that battery of red hot fireboxes in the basement going full blast to heat up that large cathedral-like church. Old Hedrick, the janitor, always seemed to be generous with the heat on Christmas and would really pour the coal into those four or five furnaces. It dawned on me later that maybe the pastor put him up to it since he wanted the people to feel very comfortable that day. You see, in those days the pastor received the Christmas collection, and if the people felt good they might peel off a green-back instead of throwing in a quarter or maybe a half.

Since the hot air registers were all in the front, if Hedrick didn't fire up full blast, the front of the church would be warm, and the back part would be cold. On ordinary Sundays that was the pastor's way of trying to freeze out the young bucks who always took the rear pews away from the mothers and babies who had first right to them.

But on Christmas everybody was warm. And to see those furnaces glowing red hot early Christmas morning was the highlight of the Feast for this little pagan.

In 1934 it was still common enough for people to travel to church with horse-drawn sleighs. Cars were often hard to start, but what was more troublesome was the difficulty of keeping sufficient alcohol antifreeze in the radiators. Those of us who have had the experience of driving to church in the dark on Christmas morn in a sleigh somehow never forget it, especially on those quiet winter nights when the stars seem to be so close to the earth, and is there a night when they seem closer than on Christmas?